the
Incredible
Bread
Machine

WORLD RESEARCH, INC.
CAMPUS STUDIES INSTITUTE DIVISION
11722 Sorrento Valley Road
San Diego, California 92121

Distributed by:
Ward Ritchie Press
474 S. Arroyo Parkway
Pasadena, California 91105

THE INCREDIBLE BREAD MACHINE

Based on a book of the same title by R.W. Grant, first published in 1966. The present edition has been updated and extensively revised by the student staff of Campus Studies Institute under the supervision of Patty Newman, CSI Senior Editor and Director of Program Development.

SUSAN LOVE BROWN
KARL KEATING
DAVID MELLINGER
PATREA POST
STUART SMITH
CATRIONA TUDOR

Cover design
by
PAM PSIHOS

1st Printing — Oct. 1, 1974
2nd Printing — Nov. 15, 1974
3rd Printing — Feb. 20, 1975
4th Printing — Apr. 21, 1975
5th Printing — March 15, 1976
6th Printing — March 15, 1977
7th Printing — March 15, 1978

Spanish Language Edition

1st Printing — Dec. 1976

Library of Congress Catalogue Card Number 74-80968

CONTENTS

PREFACE

Global economic instability, a widespread decline in personal freedom, and our own desire for job security* "persuaded" us to write this book.

We wish to thank Richard Grant for the use of his book as a basis for and guide in discussing these issues. We also wish to thank CSI Senior Editor Patty Newman for her sarcasm, obstinance, and bullying, without which this book would have come out much sooner (and much worse).

Susan Love Brown (age 26)
Karl Keating (24)
David Mellinger (23)
Patrea Post (23)
Stuart Smith (25)
Catriona Tudor (23)

*Our resumes on request if this book flops.

WHEAT FROM CHAFF

It was April and the ground was still too wet for plowing, so farmer Valentine Byler decided to haul rocks to fill a mudhole in his lane. He hitched his two bay mares to an old flatboat. Then he hitched the colt with them to help get it broken in. A short time later two strangers approached. "This isn't going to be pleasant," said one of them. They took the reins. Byler was Amish and his religious beliefs forbade him to resist. The two men unhitched the team. "I couldn't watch," said Byler, "I went into the woods." The men led the horses away.

The men were agents of the Internal Revenue Service. For reasons of religious conviction Byler had refused to pay his Social Security taxes and the horses were seized to satisfy the government claim. On May 1, 1961, the IRS sold the two mares and the colt at auction for $460. The IRS took $308.96 for back taxes and $113.15 for "expenses." Byler got back $37.89.[1]

When the State, under the pretext of caring for people, takes away from them the means by which they might care for themselves, does such legislation represent a step forward or a step back? This episode dramatizes some rather fundamental issues.

In and out of Congress there was a great deal of criticism of the IRS action, and in March of 1965 the IRS abruptly announced that the Amish would no longer be forced to participate in the Social Security program.

If the Amish are to be excused from participation because of their religious convictions and if others are to be denied this option unless their religion corresponds to that of the Amish, is this not the application by the IRS of a religious test? Is the IRS going to declare that the convictions of the Amish are more pure than those of other religions? Has not the Supreme Court declared repeatedly that such tests are unconstitutional?

What about government activities other than the Social Security programs? Should not support for these be placed on a voluntary basis for those who object on the moral premise involved? How are questions like this to be decided?

Consider the 1964 case of a Los Angeles resident named Steven Anthony who refused to vacate his home which had been condemned by Los Angeles County under the laws of eminent domain. The land was to be turned over to a private group for the construction of the Hollywood Motion Picture and Television Museum. For ten weeks Anthony barricaded himself in his home holding off with a shotgun the deputies who sought to evict him. Finally, two plain clothes policemen gained access by posing as sympathizers. Anthony was arrested and jailed. The next day the house was demolished by court order. The judge labeled this previously unknown man "an anarchist, a rabble rouser, and a publicity seeker" and sentenced him to a year in jail for battery and resisting arrest.*[2]

But who was really the guilty party? Was Anthony the aggressor or the victim of aggression? Was he violating someone's rights, or was he seeking to hold what was rightfully his? Was the law used in this case to protect rights or to violate them? Is it proper that the State seize private property for the construction of a privately operated museum? Would the issue be different if the museum were to have been publicly operated?

---

*All plans for building the movie museum have been abandoned due to dissention among the ranks of the Hollywood promoters. The property is currently being used as a parking lot.

Or consider the case of Samuel McBride. During the height of the energy crisis, the IRS channeled considerable resources and time into catching gas station operators who initiated ways of charging more for their gasoline than the government thought fit.

One of the first targets of bureaucratic fire was a Chicago independent station owner named Samuel McBride. McBride was giving away gas, with a small condition: The gas was free *if* the interested customer would first purchase for $10.50 a rabbit's foot or a legal will form.[3] There was no force or fraud involved; the terms for receiving his gasoline were completely in the open. In spite of the fact that some people, of their own free will, wanted to deal with McBride (perhaps they figured that gas at $2.00 a gallon was better than no gas at 53.9 cents a gallon, or perhaps they felt their time could be spent more valuably at work than waiting in long lines), the IRS agents charged McBride with price gouging and the court fined him $17,000.

Should the choice to deal or not to deal with Samuel McBride have been taken from the people? Should that decision be made arbitrarily by our government?

Suppose you are asleep in your own home. In the middle of the night you hear strange noises, but before you can investigate your bedroom door is kicked in and shabbily clad, unshaven men burst in shouting obscenities and waving guns. They proceed to ransack your home, destroy your property, and threaten your life.

It is not 1984, and they are not members of the Orwellian "Thought Police." They are members of the United States Justice Department's Office of Drug Abuse and Law Enforcement, and they are there to do their duty.

That scene happened to two residents of Collinsville, Illinois, in late 1973. According to testimony, these federal officers never satisfactorily identified themselves or explained the nature of their authority or showed a search warrant. In fact, they were in the *wrong* house altogether.

Charges were filed by the victims, seeking to recover damages to compensate for the destruction of their property. However, the case was lost and the government agents were acquitted.[4]

PART ONE

A prize cartoon depicted Smith
With fat and drooping jowls
Snatching bread from hungry babes
Indifferent to their howls.

CHAPTER ONE

THE BREAD ALSO RISES

Most people point to nineteenth century American capitalism as a period in which unprincipled men — the "robber barons" — seized control of vital areas of the economy and exacted tribute from an entire nation. It was a perfect example of a savage and ruthless dog-eat-dog system. The capitalists were the exploiters; the rest of the nation the exploited. They say this was "laissez faire capitalism" and it was a system that did not work. It led to fraud, depredation, corruption, ruin, and despair. There was unrestrained competition on the one hand and monopoly on the other — both were bad. A few men made millions of dollars at the expense of many — at a prohibitive cost in human dignity and in the nation's moral and spiritual values.

The Railroads. The Erie Ring. The Credit Mobilier. Vanderbilt. J.J. Hill. The Octopus of California. The "Big Four." Rockefeller. The Standard Oil Trust. All bad and all the consequence of unrestrained "laissez faire capitalism."

It was not until an aroused public demanded government regulation; not until the laws, the control, the bureaus were created; not until then did the economy serve the many rather than the few. The Interstate Commerce Act. The Sherman Antitrust Act. The Clayton Act. Gradually, government participation began to bring order out of the chaos and social justice out of the economic tyranny of the "robber barons."

This is history as taught in our schools, acted upon in our Congress, and believed by the man in the street.

But is it true? Is it possible that the multitude of evils attributed to nineteenth century American capitalism arose not because of this system, but because of government interference? Is it possible that this nation never really had laissez faire capitalism?

Laissez faire capitalism is an economic system of voluntary exchange between individuals without interference from the government.

From the start the United States economy was riddled with government intervention of many kinds: subsidies, franchises, special privileges and political favors.

For instance, in his book, *Throttling the Railroads*, Clarence B. Carson says: ". . . the railroads are the classic example in American history of the impact of government intervention on a business . . . except for banking and the delivery of the mails, the railroads have probably the longest history of [government] intervention of any major business in the United States. Nor is there any better place to study the debilitating effects of this."[1]

There were several reasons why the government became involved in the building of railroads in the nineteenth century. First of all, many people felt there was a dire need in America for more efficient transportation. The bounds of the United States had been stretched further west by the Treaty of Paris in 1783 and by the Louisiana Purchase in 1803. Fearing the impending competition from cities in the Mississippi River Valley, the eastern seaboard cities had to find a way to link up with the Midwest, and there was an urgent push for government aid in the areas of road building. Many of the early railroad lines were actually the projects of state governments (the Pennsylvania Railroad, for example), but the great transcontinental lines were where the federal government focused its attentions. Carson explains that government aid was extended on the grounds that private investors were probably reluctant at this time to put up sufficient money for building roads, because, in actuality, there was no market for these railroads (had there been, the private investors would have undertaken to provide them). "Though private investors might have been wrong," says Carson, "they are the experts in the field. Governments are betting against the field when they put up money."[2]

In 1934 Matthew Josephson wrote an influential book called *The Robber Barons.* The theme of Josephson's book is that capitalism caused and government cured the excesses of the nineteenth century. However, on close examination, Josephson's book actually shows that the real villain was government intervention — not capitalism.

Consider, for example, one of the more infamous frauds in U.S. history—that of the Credit Mobilier, a uniquely conceived "construction" company owned by those who controlled the Union Pacific Railroad. Capitalism has received the blame for what happened, but what Josephson describes is surely not capitalism:

In short order the Pacific Railroad bill was passed [1862], and the two companies which undertook the colossal affair were given federal charters. The Union Pacific, building westward from the Missouri River, was granted 12,000,000 acres of unknown land, in alternate sections ten miles deep, and also $27,000,000 in six percent, thirty-year government bonds as a first mortgage. The Central Pacific, building from the sea eastward to meet the Union Pacific, was similarly granted 9,000,000 acres of land and $24,000,000 in government bonds.[3]

This was how the Credit Mobilier promoters got their capital: not by private investment, but by government subsidy. Subsidies, franchises, land grants and associated government involvements which are not characteristics of laissez faire capitalism. In addition, the affair had the political benediction of both parties. And with booty like this at stake, the result was inevitable. The men who became involved were not interested in building a railroad — they were out to milk it dry. Through the Credit Mobilier they subcontracted to themselves the actual construction work. The costs to the railroad mysteriously skyrocketed, while the profits to the Credit Mobilier were immense, and when the true nature of the vast swindle became known:

> . . . the tale of appalling waste, of crime and turpitude shook the whole country like a mighty quake and set many a weak structure to rocking . . . thousands lost their savings in Union Pacific's fall, while distress spread quickly to the grain-growing regions. From the rostrum the tribunes of the people . . . began to speak out, in tones soon to become familiar whenever such provocation arose, *against the giant corporations which overran the country* . . . [emphasis added] [4]

Josephson also mentions the famous fight in 1872 for control of the Erie Railroad. Jay Gould, Jim Fisk, and old Daniel Drew were possibly scoundrels without peer. Their victim was the Erie. Josephson writes:

> The Erie was then a great trunk line, nearly 500 miles long, plying between the harbor of New York and the Great Lakes. It had been built at a cost of $15,000,000 partly through state subsidies... Its rickety, lamp-lit trains, its weak iron rails had brought disaster and scandal, such as clung to its whole career; and when Daniel Drew, by virtue of his loans to the company, became its treasurer and master after the panic of 1857, it was soon clear that the flinty master was not in the least interested in the Erie Railroad as a public utility or highway of traffic.
>
> His strategic position gave him intimate knowledge of the large railroad's affairs which he used only to advance his private speculations. The very decrepitude of the rolling stock, the occurrence of horrendous accidents, were a financial "good" to the Speculative Director, who used even the treasury of his railroad to augment his short selling of its own stock. . . .
>
> Gould and Fisk were soon "insiders" who might know in advance when the Erie shares would rise or fall, and smiling times began for them. Only a single cloud disturbed the busy gentlemen of the Erie Ring; it was the ponderous encroachments of a berserk force

in the railroad field, the aged Cornelius Vanderbilt, whose seemingly resistless advance
menaced them all with extinction.[5]

In a free economy if a company is misman-
aged, an opposition group of stockholders can
gain control. It was the redoubtable Commodore
Vanderbilt who led the opposition to the Erie
Ring. Vanderbilt was no mere "freebooter," he
was a builder. This remarkable man had already
amassed eleven-million-dollars when, at 68, he
fashioned from a conglomeration of lesser roads
the famous New York Central — in its day the
most extensive railroad system in the world.
What Vanderbilt touched turned to gold, for he
ran his properties efficiently and profitably. Day
after day Vanderbilt bought heavily of Erie stock,
seeking a controlling interest. Yet, it seemed,
the more he bought the more appeared on the
market — fresh, brand new shares. The Erie Ring
— now under the masterful direction of Jay
Gould — was printing stock certificates faster
than Vanderbilt could buy them.

This, of course, was a simple case of fraud,
and Vanderbilt sought an injunction. Had the
government of New York performed its proper
function of punishing fraud, Drew and Fisk and
Gould would have been restrained. But it was
Vanderbilt who was finally defeated — not by
the Erie Ring, however, but by the "gentlemen"
of the New York State legislature. These "public

servants" passed a special law legalizing the Ring's actions.

One can sympathize with the victimized Erie stockholders. Had Vanderbilt gained control, their investment undoubtedly would have been saved and the Erie would have been turned into a profitable line — profitable for the stockholders and profitable for the public. As it was, the Erie had by now been so thoroughly looted that it was unable to pay another dividend for sixty-nine years. Yet Josephson makes no distinction between Vanderbilt and the men of the Erie Ring. To Josephson, all were "robber barons." Moreover, many people today cite such episodes as the "Fight for the Erie" as horrible examples of dog-eat-dog laissez faire capitalism. But it was not capitalism that delivered the coup-de-grace to the Erie. It was the New York State legislature.

In contrast to the government-financed Union Pacific and the scoundrels of the Erie Ring was James Jerome Hill's Great Northern Railway System, a line that extended from Chicago to the Pacific coast. Hill's railroad was unique in that it was developed without any government subsidies or land grants. Josephson describes Hill:

> This aggressive figure, who seemed to have roused himself in middle age, saw things in a large way. In his conquering march through the Northern territories, he developed new methods of business, departing widely from the petty merchantilism of

the age which preceded his. He wrote to his partner Lord Mount Stephen his plain view: "It is our best interest to give low rates and do all we can to develop the country and create business." This was no mere philanthropic intention; he labored for large volume rather than for small orders at high rates. He was "sounder" and by far more "efficient" than his confreres in this business; and he ended by becoming something of an engineer himself. It is characteristic of him that although when he came into the railroad business the locomotives, like resplendent pet animals, bore names, Hill gave them numbers, doubled their tractive power until his road had the most powerful engines, the longest trains. In the same way he laid his roadbeds only after the most exhaustive surveys of grades and curves. The bridge he threw over the Mississippi between St. Paul and the present Minneapolis was one of the most massive granite structures ever made at the time...[6]

James Jerome Hill spread his railroad through Dakota and Montana, often riding ahead to spy out "unknown country at his personal risk, camping in the open, studying soil, water, climate, resources." He succeeded in meeting his competition by providing better service and by exercising shrewd business judgment. When competing railroads failed through mismanagement, Hill was accused of being a monopolist and damned without mercy along with unscrupulous managers.

Yet, his railroad was honestly run and was profitable to the stockholders and to the nation. The Great Northern was operated without government subsidy and was more successful than those that were.

In contrast, the Central Pacific—a heavily subsidized railroad — was building eastward at the same time that the Union Pacific was building westward. With its subsidiary, the Southern Pacific, it quickly became a symbol of all of the evils popularly attributed to capitalism. The Central Pacific ("The Octopus," as it was later called) soon held all of California in an iron grip. The Central Pacific had a total monopoly in the state and charged rates which were ruinously high — so high that a group of hardware merchants once calculated that it would be cheaper to transport a keg of nails from New York by shipping it around Cape Horn (the tip of South America) to California, rather than pay for the Central Pacific connection on the end of the more direct overland route.[7]

The monopoly of the Central Pacific was not the result of efficient competition and good service. It was not achieved through the mechanism of a free market, but by legislative action. The directors of the Central Pacific — the "Big Four" (Huntington, Stanford, Crocker, and Hopkins) — controlled the legislature of California. And the legislature saw to it that the Central Pacific received no competition, by refusing to let other railroads operate in the area.   Competing lines were forbidden access to any of the California ports. Had this nation truly had a capitalistic economy, this type of government "regulation" would have been constitutionally forbidden, and the Central Pacific monopoly would never have been established by fiat.

The railroads were not the only target of criticism among the earliest business ventures in America. Consider, for example, the historical treatment afforded John D. Rockefeller, the founder of Standard Oil — the nation's first "trust."

In the years prior to Standard Oil, those who could not afford the costly whale oil did without lamplight, for kerosene was still the fuel of the future. It was not until 1859 that Edwin L. Drake's famous gusher at Titusville, Pennsylvania revolutionized the fuel industry. In the early 1860's the oil industry which Rockefeller was soon to dominate was still tiny, disorganized and chaotic — production was low, crude prices fluctuated wildly and the refined product was scarce and expensive. When Rockefeller first took notice of this brawling industry, it was little more than ramshackle derricks and wild-eyed men. However, two years later, he invested $5,000 with the talented Samuel Andrews for the construction of a refinery. With a superior product and superior organizational skill, Rockefeller's enterprise steadily expanded until it became the leader in the field.

The criticism most often levelled against Rockefeller centered on his ability to undersell the competition by getting secret reductions in rates from the railroads. This procedure was largely responsible for the 1887 passage of the Interstate Commerce Act. Yet, rebates were an integral and legitimate part of railroad economy. By exacting them, Rockefeller was able to get lower rates, and it was ultimately the consumer who gained.*

What were the reformers of railroad practices asking for when they began to request government regulation of railroads? Justice? Carson says:

> To be just means, so far as I can make out, to give each man his due. In economic terms, it means that a man should have what he has earned or what has been given him by someone who earned it. So long as the railroads provided the service for which they were paid and at the rate agreed upon with each party to a contract, there would appear to be no further question of justice at issue. That is, the practices charged against the railroads could be dismissed simply as involving no instance of violation of contract. If they had, anyone unjustly treated by violation of contract would have recourse to the courts. No new laws were needed to provide such justice.

*See *Throttling the Railroads* by Clarence B. Carson, pg. 52-63. (Copyrighted 1971. Distributed by Foundation for Economic Education, Irvington on the Hudson, New York.)

What the reformers have sought, however, has not been justice. It is sometimes
called distributive justice, but it should be
called, instead, *equality*. . . . [8]

Consider the consequences of such an "equality" when put into economic practice by the railroads. First of all, in order to do this it would be
necessary to "figure how much it costs to transport a given unit a certain distance and then appor-
tion this among the customers according to the
number of units and distance shipped. . . . Of
course, no such calculation can be made. More
precisely, if such a calculation were made it
would spread disaster in every direction when
applied. It could only be an *average* cost per-
unit per-distance which would only by sheer
luck be the actual cost of shipping one unit a
given distance. *If such an average cost were then
prescribed, it might be expected to bankrupt
every railroad in the country* not only because
the costs of providing rail service vary from one
line to another and on the same line but also because they run counter to the whole purpose of
the railroad. This is why the government programs have had such a deleterious effect; not
because the programs have ever involved so sim-
plistic an approach as the above but because
they have worked off modifications of it which
ignored the nature of the services railroads
perform." [9] (Emphasis added)

It would be a mistake to assume that every nineteenth century businessman was an "architect of progress," but it is also a mistake to assume that government intrusion into the economy stimulated competition and benefited the consumer. To the extent that government interference was kept minimal, the economy prospered.

The "evils" that critics point out as justifying regulation — pools, conspiracies, rebates, and price-fixing — were without a doubt a widespread practice among businessmen during the period. But these "evils" of the free market system failed to give those businessmen control of the market. The relative absence of government controls enabled new competitors to spring up, and in the end it was the consumer who benefited.

The inherent nature of the free-market precluded continual domination of an industry. There was only one way for a business to rid itself of competition and bar entry of competitors into the market — by bringing government into the picture. On its own, big business could do nothing to stop someone from competing. Dr. Benjamin A. Rogge describes why:

> . . . the real nature of competition is the competition between the man who had the last idea and got way out ahead and the man who has come up with the new idea;

in other words, competition is a never end-
ing game of leapfrog. This is the real nature
of competition and it makes no difference
whether you have one firm, two firms, or
six firms. It makes no difference how much
money they're making at a given moment
of time. . . . Time and tide will take care of
everything — time and tide in the form of
this leapfrogging process, of somebody coming up with a new idea leapfrogging over
the old.[10]

Business realized it could not halt competition
by "cut-throat" procedures. Now it had to turn
to legislation to accomplish what a free market,
by its intrinsic nature, would not permit. As
Gabriel Kolko comments in his book, *The Triumph of Conservatism:*

All the efforts of Morgan and the cor-
porate promoters to introduce economic
stability and control over various industries,
and the bane of destructive and unprofit-
able competition, were heading toward
failure . . . The dominant fact of American
political life at the beginning of this cen-
turn was that big business led the struggle
for the regulation of the economy. . . . Nor
was it possible for many businessmen to
ignore the fact that, in addition to sanctions
the federal government might provide to
ward off hostile criticisms, the national government was still an attractive potential
source of windfall profits, subsidies, and
resources.[11]

The politician also had something to gain by this liaison between government and the economy. After the Erie Ring and Credit Mobilier scandals, politicians had reaped the ire of the public. It became advantageous to the politicians to disassociate themselves with such enterprises. The tack that politicians used was simple:

> It was to shift the onus from politics to business, to expose businessmen as malefactors and reveal politicians as guardian angels. . . . What an individual politician could do would be to vote against the railroads and establish his innocence of bribery. A vote to contain, obstruct, and restrict big business could be worn as a badge of innocence.[12]

This is a practice which politicians have retained to the present day. With big business seeking the protection of government regulation and the politicians anxious to wear the badge of innocence, the economic burden of government intervention came into being on an even larger scale than before. Despite the ill-effects that were clearly due to such intervention, people became convinced that it was "capitalism" that had led to all the trouble.

But anticapitalist bias did not originate in America. Capitalism has had a very bad press everywhere. From the outset, the Industrial Revolution in England as well as in the United States was regarded by the major portion of the intellectual community as an invention of the devil. The misconceptions of yesterday do not die easily; they usually end up comprising the conventional wisdom of today.

Several generations of eighteenth- and nineteenth-century writers, clergymen, and assorted social critics tended to lay the blame for every social woe, real or imagined, at the factory doorstep. Many of the intellectuals during the Industrial Revolution looked about and suddenly noticed that there was poverty. But the poverty had been there all along. Why, then, the passionate distaste for the very system which was gradually improving man's material lot? Possibly capitalism was its own worst enemy in this respect, for in raising the general standard of living it made more conspicuous the poverty that still remained. Whatever the explanation, industrialization was roundly denounced from the rostrums and pulpits and in the newspapers.

Child labor was a particular target of the early reformers. William Cooke Taylor wrote at the time about those reformers who, witnessing children at work in the factories, thought to themselves: "How much more delightful would have been the gambol of the free limbs on the hillside; the sight of the green mead with its spangles of buttercups and daisies; the song of the bird and the humming of the bee. . . . " [13] But for many of these children the factory system meant quite literally the only chance for survival. Today, we overlook the fact that death from starvation and exposure was a common fate prior to the Industrial Revolution, for the precapitalist economy was barely able to support the population. Yes, children were working. Formerly they would have starved. It was only as goods were produced in greater abundance at lower cost that men could support their families without sending their children to work. It was not the reformer or the politician that ended the grim necessity for child labor; it was capitalism.

Anticapitalist writers in nineteenth-century England were particularly repulsed by the drab and dilapidated conditions in housing. But the State was not helping matters. T.S. Ashton points out that, because of the usury law, one of the principal reasons for the shortage of workingmen's housing was the great difficulty encountered by builders in borrowing the needed money. Moreover, brick was subject to heavy tax, while the duty on the higher grade Baltic timber was all but prohibitive. The heavy hand of the bureaucrat did little to stimulate progress. Ashton comments:

> If the towns were ridden with disease, some at least of the responsibility lay with legislators who, by taxing windows, put a price on light and air and, by taxing bricks and tiles, discouraged the construction of drains and sewers. Those who dwell on the horrors that arose from the fact that the

products of the sewers often got mixed up with the drinking water, and attribute this, as all other horrors, to the Industrial Revolution, should be reminded of the obvious fact that without the iron pipe, which was one of the products of that revolution, the problem of enabling people to live a healthy life together in towns could never have been solved.[14]

Professor W.H. Hutt, who relates the episode of the 1832 "Sadler Committee Report," concludes that tendentious writings also characterized the period. Sadler was endeavoring to gain Parliamentary passage of a bill limiting the working day to ten hours, and to that end Parliament established a committee headed by Sadler to investigate the widespread reports of gross cruelties in factories. The one-sided report was as inaccurate as it was sensational. Even Karl Marx's colleague, Friedrich Engels, described the Sadler Report as "emphatically partisan, composed by strong enemies of the factory system for party ends. Sadler permitted himself to be betrayed by his noble enthusiasm into the most distorted and erroneous statements . . . "[15]

The Sadler Report, filled with stories of brutality, degradation and oppression, was immensely influential. It became the bible for indignant reformers well into the twentieth century. The Hammonds describe it as "one of the main sources of our knowledge of the conditions

of factory life at the time. Its pages bring before
the reader in vivid form of dialogue the kind of
life that was led by the victims of the new
system."[16] Hutchins and Harrison describe it as
"one of the most valuable collections of evidence on industrial conditions that we possess."[17]

One suspects that much of the anticapitalist
bias of today could be traced back to the fire-
breathing,   nineteenth-century reformers like
Sadler. Were Bertrand Russell and Matthew Josephson influenced by the Sadler Report, or by
the works of the Hammonds or of Hutchins and
Harrison? No doubt that influence was considerable And no doubt that influence has extended
as well to Schlesinger, Galbraith, Theobald,
and the other intellectuals who find the answers
to all problems in a planned economy and
collectivism

CHAPTER TWO

THE SUN SINKS IN THE YEAST

The misconception that the "robber barons" came to power because of the lack of government regulation has become an economic tenet. Equally well-rooted in our contemporary economic philosophy is that boom-and-bust business cycles are characteristic of capitalism. Most people believe that capitalism led to the Great Depression.

Without question this view of capitalism is shared by the great majority of the American people, even many professing to be "free-enterprisers." But are these accusations grounded in historical fact? Are fluctuating periods of prosperity and depression actually inherent traits of a free market?

There are as many theories of the business cycle as there are economists to argue about it, but perhaps the most cohesive and consistent interpretation was espoused by the renowned economist, Professor Ludwig von Mises.

THE GREAT DEPRESSION: THE MISESIAN THEORY

A tendency toward instability is not an inherent characteristic of laissez faire capitalism. In fact, a money market free from government intervention provides the ideal economic stabilizer: the interest rate. It is like a sign post pointing out to the businessman the direction that he should take.

What low interest rates indicate: If interest rates are low, this is an indication that people are willing to lend; they are willing to forego immediate consumption for the sake of future profits. For example, an individual might forego the purchase of a new refrigerator today in order to save his money to build a home ten years from now. Instead of spending his money on consumer goods, he puts it in the bank. This money now becomes available for loans to businessmen. If this consumer preference is shared by tens of thousands of others, money for lending purposes will be abundant and interest rates will fall. When interest rates are low, businessmen are encouraged to take out long-term loans and develop long-term capital goods such as steel mills, railroads, and land.   These undertakings will not come to fruition for years, but when they do, a market will exist because those original consumers are now finally ready to build those houses. The developed land is ready and waiting, the steel mills can supply the nails, and the railroads can haul the lumber. The low interest rates have resulted in an economic structure appropriate to the long-term desires of the consuming public.

What high interest rates indicate: If interest rates are high, it is an indication that money for lending is in short supply. Perhaps an excessive amount of loans has already been made, people are reluctant to lend because of political instability, economic conditions simply do not warrant optimism, people have tied up money in home purchases rather than waiting to buy them at a later date. Whatever the reason, the higher rates automatically discourage investment in long-term capital goods for which no secure market will exist.

The interest rate indicates to the businessman the direction his investment should take. Suppose the rates should be high but are held at artificially low levels by some kind of government intervention, such as artificial credit expansion? The signals have been switched. As a result excessive investment will occur, particularly in capital goods. This is "malinvestment," i.e., investment in the wrong things. The day of reckoning can be postposed by further credit expansion, but it cannot be evaded permanently, for businessmen have made investments that cannot be successfully integrated into the economy. These ventures must finally cease operation. Workers will be laid off, and the effects will quickly percolate down to the consumer-goods industries as well. The depression has begun.

Thus the credit structure (in terms of the interest rate) constitutes the automatic signal for economic activity. Time and again this signal has been tampered with by government. Artificial credit expansion might be caused by direct government control of credit, or it might arise from the issuance of unsound currency. In any case the result of this monetary inflation will be an interest rate held at an artificially low level, thus setting the stage for a boom-and-bust cycle.

This country's major depressions started in 1837, 1873, 1892, and 1929. In each case, in accordance with von Mises' theory, the bust was preceded by several years of government-inspired inflation of one kind or another. Prior to the crash of 1837 the principal mechanism was the issuance of unsound paper currency by the various state banks. The bust of 1873 was preceded by the government-managed inflation attending the Civil War. The crash of 1892 was generated in part by the issuance of silver notes. The Great Depression of the thirties was preceded by a decade of inflation generated for the most part by the Federal Reserve System – the "Fed."

There were other factors in these boom-and-bust cycles, but in each case the central ingredient has been credit expansion resulting from some form of government intervention. This is not to say that business fluctuations would not take place otherwise, for businessmen will often guess wrong, make mistakes, and will invest too deeply in the wrong place at the wrong time. Even in a free economy dislocations will occur and adjustments will be necessary. But the effect will be local and short-lived. With the inexorable push of deliberate government policy, the entire economy usually finds itself swept along on a nation-wide wave of speculation that builds higher and higher – and then collapses.

THE GREAT DEPRESSION: WHAT CAUSED IT

The Great Depression did not "just happen." Nor did it start in 1929. The groundwork was laid years before.

The Federal Reserve System, created by law

in 1913, was to be a central bank from which bankers could draw funds in times of stress. But prior to 1913 private bankers had always been ready to pool their resources to support those who merited support. It would have been better had the nation's monetary system continued to evolve in private hands, for the Federal Reserve System proved to be an engine of inflation that crippled the nation's economy.

Between June, 1921, and June, 1929, the nation's money supply (currency plus currency substitutes, such as bank deposits) increased by a startling 62% from 45.3 billion to 73.3 billion dollars.[1] The nature of the government-controlled fractional reserve banking system is such that this $28 billion increase was generated by a much smaller increase in bank reserves, and this increase in bank reserves was generated by the Fed. In explaining the mechanism of the fractional reserve banking system and the effect of Fed policy on the money supply, a Federal Reserve System pamphlet comments:

The Federal Reserve System is the only instrumentality endowed by law with discretionary power to create (or extinguish) the money that serves as bank reserves or as the public's pocket cash. Thus, the ultimate capability for expanding or reducing the economy's supply of money rests with the Federal Reserve.[2]

In short, the Federal Reserve controls the money supply by manipulating bank reserves. The mechanisms by which bank reserves were manipulated by the Federal Reserve in the years prior to the Great Depression were: low rediscount rates, open market purchase of government securities, and extensive purchase of acceptances — all of which constituted a cheap money policy.*

The reasons for this policy were to "help business," to encourage foreign loans, and to save England from the consequences of its own heavy inflation.

First, by easing credit, it was expected that business prosperity could be encouraged and maintained. Secretary of the Treasury William McAdoo explained the Fed's easy-money:

> The primary purpose of the Federal Reserve Act was to alter and strengthen our banking system that the enlarged credit resources demanded by the needs of business and agricultural enterprises will come almost automatically into existence and at rates of interest low enough to stimulate, protect and prosper all kinds of legitimate business. [3]

Second, foreign loans would supposedly supply

---

*For more information on the cheap money policy see Murray Rothbard's *America's Great Depression* and Milton Friedman's *The Great Contradiction 1929-1933.*

the money by which those countries could purchase American products, particularly agricultural. American agriculture was in a deep slump in the early twenties due in large part to the backlash of the highly protectionist Forney-McCumber Tariff of 1922. Unable to sell to us, Europeans had found it equally difficult to buy from us. The foreign loans would supposedly provide the Europeans with the purchasing power that the tariff had eliminated. Secretary of Commerce Hoover commented that even "bad loans" helped U.S. exports.[4] It would have been wiser to reduce tariffs rather than encourage the extension of shaky loans, but alas, this is not the way of the State even today.

Finally, perhaps the least commendable motive behind the policy of deliberate inflation was a humanitarian desire to protect England from the consequences of its own destructive cheap money policies. Great Britain was losing gold to the U.S. at an alarming rate, and the officials of the Fed sought to save the British from embarrassment by deliberately debasing our own currency. By so doing, interest rates would be forced down and capital balances would be diverted from this country to England. Dr. Benjamin Anderson, at that time economist for the Chase Manhattan Bank, writes in his book *Economics and The Public Welfare:*

The governors of the other eleven Federal Reserve banks were called to Washington [in 1927]. They were not dealt with honestly. They were told that the proposed cheap money move was to "help the farmer." They were not told that the primary purpose of it was to make it unnecessary for England to honor her gold obligations to France, and to make it possible for England to continue an unwarranted degree of cheap money. . . .

The Chicago Federal Reserve Bank was suspicious and disapproved. The Chicago Federal Reserve Bank was in a better position to know what was really involved in the [cheap money] policy than the Federal Reserve banks of the more remote places. The Governor of the Chicago Federal Reserve Bank had less confidence in Governor Strong than many of the other governors had. The Chicago bank refused to reduce its [rediscount] rate. But the Federal Reserve Board at Washington overrode the Chicago Federal Reserve Bank, and by action of the Board, not of the Bank, the Chicago rate was reduced . . . [5]

And so, first by one means and then another, for a period of about eight years, the Federal Reserve System fed the fires of inflation, increasing the money supply by about 62%. The principal barometer of this was the stock market. It soared to incredible heights. Whenever it threatened to sag, a timely reassurance from the Secretary of the Treasury or from President Coolidge himself was sufficient to send it on a mercurial rise.

In November of 1922 the *New York Times* average of industrial stocks stood at 108; seven years later that average surged to 381.[6] Timidly, the Fed sought to tighten up on the super-abundant credit supply. But it was much too late. The end was now in sight. It was October, 1929.

On the average day perhaps four million shares exchanged hands. On October 23, 1929, over two and a half million shares were traded in the last hour alone. The *Times* average dropped from 415 to 384. The next day was Thursday, October 24. This was Black Thursday. On this day almost thirteen million shares changed hands in a wild frenzy, as wave after wave of selling drove the market downward. But then, "organized support" appeared as leading bankers pooled their resources and stemmed the tide. Fear disappeared, and confidence returned. By the end of the day the market had recovered amazingly well, losing only 12 points, a third of the loss of the previous day. Through Friday and the half day of Saturday the market was relatively firm.

But Monday was bad; 9,250,000 shares changed hands and the *Times* industrials plummeted 49 points. This time there was no "organized support." Tuesday was worse, with an unbelievable 16,400,000 shares and a drop of another 43 points. On Wednesday, perhaps due to the words of reassurance from President Hoover's

Secretary of Commerce, the market rallied, moving up 31 points. The next day it recovered another 21 points. The market was closed Friday, Saturday, and Sunday; things were looking up — so it seemed.

On Monday the market lurched downward 22 points. Tuesday was a New York City election day and the market was closed. On Wednesday it dropped another 37 points. On Thursday and Friday the market held steady. But the first three days of the next week it lost another 50 points. It was all over.

What caused the Great Depression? It was not capitalism or "greedy businessmen" or "underconsumption" or "overproduction." Nor was it "just one of those things." It was basically government intervention, and it was the continuation of these interventionist policies during the Hoover and Roosevelt administrations which prolonged the Depression for nearly ten years.

THE GREAT DEPRESSION: WHAT PROLONGED IT

The Hoover Years

Herbert Hoover had been President only a year when the crash occurred. Perhaps the most pernicious notion within the Hoover administration was that it is high wages that cause prosperity. It followed that the way to cure a depression would be to keep wages high, even in the face of dropping prices and extinguished profits. Accordingly, as the depression deepened, action was quick. At a series of conferences in November, Hoover extracted assurances from most major business leaders that wages would not be lowered. But in a depression it is essential that excessively high wages drop just as do the excessively high prices. If wages are kept high in the face of extinguished profits, the result will be widespread business failures and soaring unemployment. That is precisely what happened.

Well into 1931 hourly wages had declined by only about 4%, while real wages had actually increased (due to falling prices) by around 11%. It was the intent of the Hoover wage policy that national "purchasing power" be kept high, but the result was the opposite, for now there were eight million unemployed.[7]

But there were other weapons in the government arsenal. Back in June of 1929, Congress had passed the Agriculture Marketing Act, by which was established the Federal Farm Board (FFB). The purpose of this board was two-fold: to make low-interest loans to farm cooperatives and to support prices. To support wheat prices the FFB established the Farmers National Grain Corporation with $10 million in government money. With an assured market at subsidized prices, the farmers grew still more wheat. Under the weight of the new surpluses, prices dropped still further and the FFB was given another $100 million with which to continue the process.[8]

In an effort to stabilize prices, the administration then established the Grain Stabilization Corporation. In an effort to reduce surpluses, the Secretary of Agriculture hopefully urged farmers to reduce acreage. Needless to say, wheat surpluses continued to pile up. The FFB had similar success with cotton. In 1931 Chairman Stone urged frantically that every third row be plowed under. By 1933 the wheat and cotton programs had cost the taxpayers $300 million.[9]

The FFB had equal "success" with wool, butter, beans, pecans, figs, grapes, raisins, potatoes, apples, sugarbeets, honey, nuts, maple syrup, tobacco, poultry, eggs, and rice. Benjamin Anderson comments: "Those who condemn the New Deal for its agricultural follies in 1933 and succeeding years . . . should not credit Roosevelt's New Deal with originality on this point."[10]

Possibly there is no economic act more insidiously harmful than a protective tariff. Yet in 1930 President Hoover signed into law the Smoot-Hawley Tariff, which imposed the highest rates in U.S. history. Anderson describes this as "the crowning financial folly of the whole period from 1920 to 1933." On the day the bill was passed, the hard-pressed stock market shuddered in agony and dropped 20 points. The

Smoot-Hawley Tariff triggered a wave of destructive protectionism all around the world and international trade was all but crippled.

The administration called for an "ample supply of credit at low rates" (more inflation) and urged a further increase in public works. In February of 1931 President Hoover signed into law a one-billion-dollar public works bill, the Employment Stabilization Act. In 1932 the weary economy was burdened further by sharply increasing taxes. The major achievement of the year, however, was the creation of the Reconstruction Finance Corporation (RFC), the purpose of which was to make loans to shaky businesses — businesses too unsound to merit private support.

A depression is caused by malinvestment — by investment in capital goods for which no real demand exists. It is only when capital is withdrawn from these areas and reinvested in useful things that recovery can ensue. Programs such as the RFC, in propping up unsound positions, served only to delay the liquidations and readjustments without which recovery was impossible. Nonetheless, in 1932 the scope of the RFC was broadened still further to embrace loans to agriculture and to cities and states for relief and public works.

There were now 12 million unemployed.[11] The nation's first federal relief program was passed in 1932. During this period the Fed continued the heavy purchase of government securities in order to increase bank reserves, thereby inflating the money supply again. By now worried banks were reluctant to lend to their full legal limit. This was one of the major reasons the administration's attempt to generate still more inflation was frustrated. Angrily, RFC Chairman Atlee Pomerene declared: "Now . . . and I measure my words, the bank that is 75% liquid or more and refuses to make loans when proper security is offered, under present circumstances is a parasite on the community."

Twelve million men, representing 25% of the working force, were unemployed in 1932. [12] Hoover's term was over. He had indeed resorted to, in his words as he accepted his Party's renomination, "the most gigantic program of economic defense and counter-attack ever evolved in the history of the Republic." This gigantic program of government intervention was a tragic failure.

The Roosevelt Years

Many procapitalists had good reason to be disenchanted with the Hoover administration, and in Franklin D. Roosevelt they thought they saw prospects for a quicker return to economic sanity. During the campaign Roosevelt had promised a balanced budget, a 25% cut in government spending, adherence to the gold standard, and an end to the proliferation of government bureaus. In his words: "Were it possible to find 'master minds' so unselfish, so willing to decide unhesitatingly against their own personal interest or private prejudices, men almost god-like in their ability to hold the scales of justice with an even hand, such a government might be to the interest of the country, but there are none such on our political horizon, and we cannot expect a complete reversal of all the teachings of history."[13] This was heartening stuff, and many people worked actively in his behalf.

It came as a great surprise then when the New Deal further exposed the nation to the delights of the managed economy. Much has been said about going off the gold standard, but of more lasting significance was the actual seizure of privately held gold. When there exist no restrictions on the ownership and use of gold, people are ultimately free to accept or reject paper money depending on their assessment of the integrity of those who have issued it. Private ownership of gold represented a potential road block to New Deal economic controls. Accordingly, the administration quickly set about to acquire physical possession and legal title to all gold in the nation.

Immediately upon taking office Roosevelt achieved passage of the Emergency Banking Relief Act (March 9, 1933), granting to the administration wide descretionary powers over money. On April 5 this power was invoked. By Presidential Order #6102 private parties were directed, under threat of heavy penalty, to exchange all gold bullion, gold coins, and gold certificates for other forms of currency. Banks were directed to deliver their gold supply to the Federal Reserve banks in exchange for credit or payment. The Federal Reserve banks in turn were to deliver the gold to the Treasury.[14]

During the previous campaign Roosevelt had endorsed "100%" a speech by Democratic Senator Glass pledging Democratic support to the gold standard. Now, with gold out of private hands, the gold standard was abandoned. The Thomas Amendment gave the President discretionary power to devalue the dollar by up to 50%. "It's dishonor, Sir," cried Senator Glass in dismay. "This great government, strong in gold, is breaking its promise to [those] to whom it has sold Government bonds with a pledge to pay gold coin of the present standard of value. It is breaking its promise to redeem its paper money in gold coin of the present standard of value. It's dishonor, Sir!"[15]

On June 5, 1933, Congress declared invalid the gold redemption clause in private contracts and in all government obligations. In other words, those who had in good faith bought government bonds redeemable in gold coin, or who held gold-backed Federal Reserve Notes, were defrauded. Senator Gore from Oklahoma said to Roosevelt: "Why, that's just plain stealing, isn't it Mr. President?"[16]

Next, in accordance with the Gold Reserve

Act of January 30, 1934, the federal government finally took legal title to all of the gold now accumulated in the Treasury, paying for it in so-called "gold certificates." These certificates failed to state just what value in gold they represented. Dr. Benjamin Anderson was one of those who testified before the Senate Committee on Banking and Currency. He writes that he protested the vague nature of these "certificates," whereupon he "was taken aside by one of the administration Senators who grinned and said, 'Doctor, you don't understand about these gold certificates. These are not certificates that you can get gold. These are certificates that gold has been taken away from you.' "[17]

With all gold now legally and physically in the hands of the State, the rest was anticlimatic. In accordance with the Gold Reserve Act the President finally devalued the dollar to a fixed level of about 60% of its original worth. The government made a clear "profit" of about $2.8 billion since the paper dollars with which it had purchased the gold were now sharply depreciated in value.[18]

The seizure of gold by the State was not only a dishonest act, it was economically self-defeating, for the appropriation of the private property of American citizens did little to restore business confidence. However, the real significance of these measures lay elsewhere. Previously, the federal government had exercised considerable control over the nation's money, but now with all gold in the hands of the State, that control was nearly total.

Prior to the final devaluation, Roosevelt's advisors ("The Brain Trust") engaged in considerable experimentation in "money management." One of the fashionable theories of the day held that the level of commodity prices could be adjusted simply by varying the gold content of the dollar.

Day by day the administration juggled the gold content of the dollar by varying the price at which the government stood ready to buy gold. It started at $31.26 an ounce. Then a little more the next day, and a little more the day after in a manner quite unrelated to the economic facts of life. Secretary of the Treasury Morganthau described years later how the day-to-day price of gold was actually arrived at:

Every morning Jesse Jones and I would meet with George Warren in the President's bedroom, to set the price of gold for the day. Franklin Roosevelt would lie comfortably on his old-fashioned three-quarter mahogany bed. . . .

The actual price . . . made little difference. . . . One day, when I must have come in more than usually worried about the state of the world, we were planning an increase of from 19 to 22 cents. Roosevelt took one look at me, and suggested a rise of 21 cents.

"It's a lucky number," the President said

with a laugh, "because it's three times seven." I noted in my diary at this time: "If anybody ever knew how we really set set the gold price . . . I think they would really be frightened." [19]

Needless to say, the scheme did not work. As usual, the government was dealing only with symptoms, not with underlying realities. The result was not to raise commodity prices but to depress economic activity. How much was a dollar worth? Would it be worth anything the next year or the year after? How could an interest rate be established? Senator Glass said in dismay, "No man outside of a lunatic asylum will loan his money on a farm mortgage."[20] But "The Brain Trust" was already prepared to fill the vacuum in private credit that their own policies had helped create. With lending organizations such as the Reconstruction Finance Corporation, the Farm Credit Administration and Home Owners Loan Corporation, the financial capital of the nation began to shift from New York City to Washington, D.C. "Washington," said Roosevelt, "has the money and is waiting for the proper projects to which to allot it."[21]

Rarely did a piece of New Deal legislation achieve its advertised goal, and all involved a still greater concentration of power in the hands of the State.

One of the more drastic programs in this re-

spect was the ill-famed National Recovery Act
(NRA). Its purpose was to set industry-by-
industry codes of minimum prices, rates, wages,
etc. It is no tribute to the business community
that some of its members, attracted by the pros-
pect of legally enforced immunity from the rigors
of competition, initially supported the act. But
this enthusiasm began to wane when it appeared
that the NRA would enforce not only rigid prices
but rigid wages, shorter hours, and increased hiring. The goal of the NRA was to increase prices
and increase purchasing power — both at the
same time.

The minimum wage policy of the NRA represented the idea that if wages could arbitrarily be
kept high, prosperity would somehow be assured.
But the sharply increased labor costs imposed an
all but intolerable burden on business. The result
was a slump in industrial production of about
25% in the six months after the NRA became
effective.[22] Minimum wage laws served to price
the marginal worker out of a job. Charles F.
Roos, at one time the Director of Research for
the NRA, estimated that its minimum wage codes
forced about one-half million blacks onto relief
in 1934.[23] He added that these provisions were
particularly harmful to the inexperienced worker
and the old worker.

NRA regimentation became so intense that
tailor Jack Magid was arrested, convicted, fined,
and sent to jail for charging thirty-five cents for

pressing a suit; the NRA code stipulated forty cents. In the famous *Schecter* case a wholesale poultry dealer was convicted for, among other things, permitting "selections of individual chickens taken from coops and half coops." This practice was a violation of the NRA "Live Poultry Code." The case finally went to the Supreme Court. The Court declared that Congress could not delegate power virtually without limit, and the entire NRA was declared unconstitutional.[24]

The Supreme Court was now striking down quite a number of New Deal measures. Accordingly, the New Deal launched an intensive propaganda campaign against the High Court. The hue and cry became "Nine Old Men." After the 1936 elections Roosevelt sought to increase the size of the Court in order to pack it with his own appointees. The Congress, which had been so compliant, finally rebelled and his plan was defeated.

It was during the New Deal years that the economic theories of British economist John Maynard Keynes came to dominate government and academic circles. He had written in 1932 in the *Yale Review*:

The decadent international but individualistic capitalism, in the hands of which we found ourselves after the war, is not a success. It is not intelligent, it is not beautiful, it is not just, it is not virtuous — and it doesn't deliver the goods. In short, we dislike it and are beginning to despise it. But when we wonder what to put in its place, we are extremely perplexed.[25]

In 1935 he summed up his views in his book, *General Theory of Employment, Interest, and Money*, which became one of the most influential books on economics ever written. Keynes' "new" economics advocated reducing the interest rates of banks in order to stimulate investment, progressive income tax to make incomes more equal (and increase the percentage of aggregate income that could be spent on consumption), and government investment in public works. This amounted to government control of the economy.

The men of the New Deal embraced the Keynesian doctrine because it lent academic respectability to those who were already dedicated to the planned economy. Did the political leaders wish to control banking? Quote John Maynard Keynes on the virtues of the "managed" currency. Did they wish to consolidate their power by means of vast federal expenditures? Quote John Maynard Keynes on the wisdom of deficit spending. Did they wish to place within their own grasp the levers and controls by which the nation's economy is operated? Quote John Maynard Keynes.

A favorite tactic was pump-priming. Billions were spent, but the net effect was not to spur recovery but to retard it, for the State can inject into the economy only what it has first taken out, either openly through taxes or surreptitiously through inflation. When government spends, the economy drinks its own blood and, in the end, is weakened accordingly. Under the stimulus of a whole catalogue of such New Deal nostrums, the economy temporarily lurched ahead in 1936 and into 1937. But a sick economy is not cured by more intervention any more than a drug addict is cured by more drugs. Late in 1937 the weary economy collapsed once again. In a nine-month period in 1937 and 1938 industrial production dropped over 34%. This was the sharpest break in the nation's history. The decline between 1929 and 1932 was deeper, but at no time was it so abrupt. The New Deal had achieved a "first": a depression within a depression. There were once again ten million unemployed.

In 1938 and 1939 Roosevelt's advisors demonstrated that they had learned little from the grim experience of the previous years. Unemployment in 1938 stood at ten million, higher than it had been in 1931. They resorted again to the destructive panaceas of pump-priming, deficit spending, and inflation.

With the outbreak of World War II the administration concentrated on one priority — all-out production for the war effort. This revived a nation that had experienced a period of government manipulation, regulation, and interference unprecedented in U.S. history.

> Economic theory demonstrates that only governmental inflation can generate a boom-and-bust cycle, and that the depression will be prolonged and aggravated by inflationist and other interventionary measures. . . . The guilt for the Great Depression must, at long last, be lifted from the shoulders of the free market economy, and placed where it properly belongs: at the doors of politicians, bureaucrats, and the mass of "enlightened" economists. And in any other depression, past or future, the story will be the same.[26]

PART TWO

True, loaves cost a dollar each
But our leaders do their best.
The selling price is half a cent
(Taxes pay the rest).

CHAPTER THREE

THE NO-DOUGH POLICY

In 1795 James Madison commented on an interesting phenomenon which he described as "the old trick of turning every contingency into a resource for accumulating force in the government." Madison knew what he was talking about

The United States never had a totally free economy, but to the extent it was free the nation prospered. As the decades passed, the controls increased in number and the distortions which resulted were used to justify the imposition of still wider controls. With the New Deal the accumulation of force continued at an accelerated rate. And it has been continuing ever since as, day by day, the bureaucrat extends his control over the economy. Controls lead to dislocations, and dislocations lead to more controls.

It is still "the old trick of turning every contingency into a resource for accumulating force in the government."

Years ago the federal government undertook to subsidize cotton farmers. But then it was discovered that the persistently high price of American cotton was hurting cotton exports. So the government subsidized exporters. But then American mill owners pointed out that foreign mills were getting American cotton cheaper than American mills could get it. So now the American mills are being subsidized. And so the growers, the exporters, and the mills are now all indebted to the State for assistance. And what the State subsidizes, to an appreciable extent it controls. "The old trick is to turn every contingency . . . "

The bureaucrat will force rates higher and then demand greater power in order to force them down again. Or, he will seek to "protect" the farmer and as a result generate a mountain of rotting surpluses; then he will demand still greater control over agriculture in order to cure the problem he himself has created. Or, he will regulate the railroads nearly into bankruptcy and then urge a program of government loans to "help" them. Or the State, through various pieces of labor legislation, will all but eliminate employer resistance to unending union demands. Then, when union power grows to ominous dimensions, labor disputes will be settled by presidential fiat rather than by free market bargaining. "Turn every contingency . . . "

MONEY

Nowhere has the old trick been more in evidence than in the ever increasing control over money. Years ago George Bernard Shaw is alleged to have observed that the voter must choose between the stability of gold and the integrity and intelligence of the Members of Parliament. "With all due respect to those gentlemen," counseled Shaw, "I advise the voter to vote for gold." This was one of Shaw's sounder political commentaries.

Only by permanent reference to a stable standard can a currency be kept sound and can the citizens of a nation protect themselves from the narcotic of politically inspired inflation. Theoretically, the money standard could be something other than gold. In fact, in some primitive societies it is cattle, shrunken heads, wives, sharks' teeth, etc. For us gold happens to be more appropriate because of its durability, limited supply, aesthetic value — in other words, global acceptance as a valued commodity.

However, some politicians and economists chafe bitterly under the impartial discipline of a gold standard. They point out that gold has no intrinsic value other than as ornamentation: "We cannot eat it or keep warm with it or patch the roof with it. Why use it? Why should the economy be disciplined by gold?" True, gold has limited intrinsic worth; its real value lies in precisely that quality to which its detractors object: Its insensitivity to political manipulation.

In a free economy people are free to accept or reject paper money depending on their assessment of the integrity of those who have issued it. Accordingly, the gold standard serves as a final check to unending inflation. Yet this nation's political leaders have sought over the past 40 years to eliminate, step by step, all metallic backing for the nation's money supply. The steps in this process have been as follows:

1.   Gold was nationalized in 1934. Private ownership of gold, except for industrial, artistic, and professional use, was forbidden.

2.   In 1945 the original requirement that the Federal Reserve banks hold a gold reserve of 35% against notes and 40% against member bank deposits was changed to 25% against notes and deposits combined. In 1964 the reserve requirement with regard to deposits was abandoned completely.

3.   In 1964 silver certificates, which were fully backed by silver or by their gold equivalent, were ordered withdrawn from circulation as rapidly as possible, to be replaced by Federal Reserve Notes.

4.   After 1965, the silver content in the nation's new coins was sharply reduced.

5. In 1968 the Federal Reserve abandoned its requirement that its notes be backed by gold. This meant that dollars could no longer be converted to gold by private foreign holders.

6. In 1971 convertibility of dollars to gold by foreign central banks was also ended.

7. U.S. experts continue to promote Special Drawing Rights as an international substitute for gold reserves — in other words, paper backed by more paper, thus virtually assuring headlong inflation on a world-wide scale.

Some of the arguments put forth in favor of a politically controlled (as opposed to a market controlled) money supply are as follows:

By its ability to influence credit, government can "bring the business cycle under control"; it can raise interest rates to damp out a boom and it can lower them to stimulate business in order to avoid a depression. But a rational examination of economic history will show that government meddling is usually the principal cause of a boom-and-bust cycle.

A second argument in behalf of government controlled money involved the assumed necessity for a steadily increasing supply. If a gold standard were adhered to, it is asked, how could the volume of money be expanded to keep pace with an expanding economy? But it is not imperative that the volume of money expand at all. If the economy expanded and the money supply did not, the value of the money unit would gradually rise, i.e., prices of things would gradually fall. And what of it? There is nothing in the stars that dictates that the volume of money must bear some fixed relationship to the size of the national product.

A third argument put forth in support of a politically controlled money supply concerns the greater ease with which government can, by means of inflation, finance its various spending programs. This spending, it is alleged, helps "keep the economy moving." But government can inject into the economy only what it has first taken out, one way or the other. An artificial increase in the number of dollars merely dilutes those already in existence. When government increases its own purchasing power via the printing press, it only diminishes the purchasing power elsewhere in the economy.

The least sophisticated but most persistent argument in support of managed money arises from the illusion that an increase in the money supply is the same thing as an increase in wealth. Money is not wealth; it is only a medium of exchange. True wealth is in the goods and services that people can actually use. If things such as food, clothing, and shelter are available in abundance, the nation is prosperous; if these things are in short supply, the nation is impoverished — money or no money. Inflation acts as a tem-

porary stimulant, but the end result is disin-
tegration.

For example, Kuwait has the highest per capita income in the world — in monetary terms.
Despite this, the country is underdeveloped and
the services and consumer products available in
other less "wealthy" countries are not available
in Kuwait. Thus, although the amount of money
held by Kuwaitians makes them "rich," the in-
ability of their market to supply products and
services causes them to be little better off than
poor countries.[1]

A fifth argument in favor of a continuation of
managed money rests on the possibility that a
halt to the associated spending and inflation
might precipitate a depression. This is certainly
possible, for the economy is suffering from a
multi-billion-dollar addiction and it is not at all
certain that withdrawal could be achieved without discomfort. However, it would seem to be
far wiser to take the cure today than to continue
on the present suicidal course. The day of reckoning can be postponed by further massive doses
of inflation, but it cannot be avoided forever.

Milton Friedman describes the situation:

In a way, it's like drink. The first few
months or years of inflation, like the first
few drinks, seem just fine. Everyone has
more money to spend and prices aren't rising quite as fast as the money that's avail-

able. The hangover comes when prices start to catch up. And, of course, some people are hurt worse than others by inflation. Some people aren't hurt at all. And others profit enormously.

When you start to take some action against inflation, on the other hand, the bad effects are felt right away. People are out of work. Interest rates go up. Money gets tight. It's unpleasant. Only later do the good effects of an end to rising prices show up. The problem is getting through the painful cure without wanting another drink. The greatest difficulty in curtailing inflation is that, after a while, people begin to think they'd rather have the sickness than the cure. What they don't realize is that once the cure has taken effect, it's possible to have both economic growth and price stability.[2]

Inflation is a source of vast political power. As John Maynard Keynes put it: "Lenin is said to have declared that the best way to destroy the capitalist system was to debauch the currency. . . . Lenin was certainly right. The process engages all the hidden forces of economic law on the side of destruction, and does it in a manner which one man in a million is able to diagnose."[3]

For just one example, during a period of inflation, wages usually rise to meet the higher cost of living. A salary raise does not mean you are making more money, because you are forced to spend more as well. In essence you are exactly where you were before the raise, *except* in one important area: *you are now in a higher income tax bracket.* In other words, *the only beneficiary of your increased salary is the government* — they are receiving more taxes from you.

But the most important area of political control that accompanies inflation is that of economic controls. Mr. Lawrence Fertig, syndicated columnist on economic affairs, points out how the sequence of events leading to the loss of freedom through inflation is similar in practically every country in the world. "First the government, through its central bank, creates conditions of easy bank credit. Also, over a period of years government spends more than it takes in, and the resulting Federal deficit is financed by creating more paper money in the banking system. This influx of new money and credit forces prices upward. Having tried to create 'Prosperity' by monetary inflation, and then finding that prices rise steeply, the government usually claims that it needs controls to curb the price increases which it has caused. It needs controls, it asserts, in order to curb the inflation which it created.... The evidence is clear. Controls, and possibly dictatorship, follow inflation as day follows night."[4]

ANTITRUST AND MONOPOLY

Suppose you have a business. Suppose you were then told (not asked) by a group of men (with the force of law behind them) that you must compete, but that you must *not* win; that you mustn't make your product so good or sell it so cheap that you obtain a dominant share of the market. What on earth would you do? If you can't produce a product that a great many people want at a price *lower* than anyone else (i.e., "win" over your competition), then why bother to go into business?

Now suppose you are a consumer. Isn't it to your advantage to have producers "competing" for your patronage? Isn't it *you* who has the most to gain by someone producing the best at the lowest cost to you? And what do you have to lose if this person, because of competition driving him to the smallest possible margin of profit, builds his business so large that he is providing the best for the least to *all* of the people?

But that's monopoly! And the government does everything within its great power to prevent it.

The Antitrust Division of the Justice Department concerns itself primarily with "conspiracies," "monopolies," and the like, while the Federal Trade Commission (FTC) directs its attentions to the "unfair trade practices" in pricing, sales practices, and so on. Such a flood of edicts, suits, precedents, decisions, regulations, and decrees have sprung from the activities of these two agencies that in 1950 Lowell Mason, maverick FTC commissioner, declared at Marquette University:

> I openly defy the entire University to explain to any businessman what he can or cannot legally do when making up his next season's price policy.
> Can he absorb freight? Perhaps, if he only does it now and then, or if he is not too big, or if the amount of the freight is not too much. But who is to say? How often is "now and then"? What size is "too big"? And how much is "too much"?
> What a young law student needs most after a diploma and a shingle and a client is a good pair of eyebrows and broad shoulders. Then when his client asks him how to stay out of trouble with the government, he can raise the first and shrug the second. . . . [5]

The cases brought to court under the antitrust laws would confuse King Solomon. *United States v. Aluminum Co.,* the Alcoa case, has been the most famous. In 1888 Alcoa produced ten pounds of aluminum daily at $8.00 a pound. By the late thirties, when the original suit was brought, the output had increased to 300 million pounds yearly, and the price had dropped to 20¢ a pound.

The trial lasted two years, and the transcript totalled over 40,000 pages. In the final analysis, the total misunderstanding of the market system, as embodied in antitrust dogma, became evident. Judge Learned Hand exemplified this basic misunderstanding, arguing in effect that Alcoa's competitiveness and superior service to the consumer in steadily reducing the cost of aluminum from dollars per pound to cents per pound was somehow bad:

> [Alcoa] insists that it never excluded competitors; but we can think of no more effective exclusion than progressively to embrace each new opportunity as it opened, and to face every newcomer with new capacity already geared into a great organization having the advantage of experience, trade connections, and the elite of personnel.[6]

This is all quite confusing. The antitrust laws were supposedly meant to protect and encourage competition, but in the process of competing it is illegal to embrace each new opportunity as it opens.   It is unfair to use your experience, trade connections, and trained personnel. That's unfair competition. What, then, *is* fair competition? Some conclude all of this is simply the impossible logic of "damned if you do and damned if you don't."

A more recent case of confusion on antitrust issues involves Firestone Tire and Rubber Company which, in August, 1973, had a suit brought against it by the United States Department of Justice in the Federal District Court in Cleveland.

According to the Firestone Annual Report, the company had purchased in 1961 the assets of Dayco Corporation's Dayton tire division and the assets of Seiberling Rubber Company's tire division in 1965:

> Both of these companies were in difficult financial condition, and had we not bought their tire businesses, many employees of these companies as well as their distributors and dealers would have suffered severe economic dislocation. The Government obviously recognized this fact at the time of the acquisitions when it took no action to prevent either one, even though the plans for each were fully disclosed to the federal antitrust enforcement officials. Now that both divisions have been rehabilitated and made profitable, the acquisitions that were not objected to before have suddenly become, in governmental retrospect, illegal steps toward monopoly.[7]

The rationale for this confusing antitrust legislation rests on misconceptions about the market system and the nature of monopolies.

For example, most people believe that when a company gets large enough it can undersell any of its small competitors and thus drive them all out of business. Then the large company can simply raise its prices again and make up for its losses by getting higher profits.

A basic law of economics is that prices are not set arbitrarily by a business, but are determined oy the demand for a product. A company will only sell a product if it can cover its expenses and expect to make a profit. If the public is not willing to pay that price for the product, the company must either lower the price, or if it cannot do that and still make a profit, go out of business. For a larger company to cut its prices to a point which would enable it to undersell a smaller competitor, it must lower the price below what it previously charged.

Although a lower price may succeed in taking customers away from the competing company, this process will take time. The larger company may have to operate at a loss or a reduced margin of profit over a period of time, still paying its normal expenses. Finally, if it did run the other company out of business and then raised its prices, it would be inviting other competitors to come into the market and sell the product at a lower price. In short, the larger company could not afford to consistently lower and raise its prices in order to eliminate competition. Not only would it be hurting itself, but it would be encouraging competition.

But some people say — and here comes another misconception — that when a company is large enough to have a monopoly, it is virtually independent of competition. In other words, they think no other business can effectively challenge it because the resources needed to compete on that level are not available.

However, a look at a 1954 Brookings Institution study, updated in 1964, would reveal that the top is a slippery place. The study by economist A.D.H. Kaplan, recalling such now-forgotten industry giants as American Locomotive, American Woolen, and American Molasses, showed that big businesses are anything but insulated from competition and fast-moving technology, that the industry colossus of one decade can become the sick firm of the next, that the "basic" industry of one era can be replaced by another "basic" industry in a new era.

Current antitrust, however, frequently tries to arrest change, to freeze the status quo, to extrapolate a static view of existing market conditions into a supposedly unalterable future. But the present as well as the future is always changing to meet ever-new economic conditions.

On the free market every company is faced with the possibility of competition, even if at a given time it appears to have a monopoly in its market. The competition will come from companies selling alternative products or newly discovered materials possibly far superior to the older products. Or it might come from the monopolist's largest customers deciding to produce the commodity themselves. For example, suppose U.S. Steel were the only steel producer and its prices were unreasonably high. There is absolutely nothing to keep the major users of steel, such as Ford, General Motors, or General Electric from manufacturing steel. These new and powerful steel producers would quickly provide a level of competition that could not readily be subdued. Consider also that Wall Street seems quite ready, willing and able to finance yet another enterprising idea, no matter how big. Capital is always seeking a profit-making investment. Smaller companies can also join forces for financial strength. In essence, no company is ever totally independent of the market — or of the consumers who comprise it.

But (continue the "misconceptionists"), can't several companies get together to set prices at a high rate forcing the consumer to pay a high price because he has no alternative?

Of course they can. And they do. But it doesn't work. Although some companies selling a similar product have tried to come to an agreement on a particular price, they have ultimately failed for two reasons. First, new competitors seize the opportunity to enter a market, which permits them to sell at a lower price and still make a profit. This, in turn, forces the other companies to lower their pre-set prices in order to compete. Secondly, and probably most importantly, one of the companies involved will drop its price just below the price agreed upon, forcing the others to do the same. Adam Smith explains that "people of the same trade seldom meet together, even for merriment and diversion, but the conversation ends in a conspiracy against the public, or in some contrivance to raise prices." But he goes on to conclude, "in a free trade an effectual combination cannot be established but by the unanimous consent of every single trader, and it cannot last longer than every single tradeı continues of the same mind."[8] In other words, human nature being what it is, the schemes usually end up in price wars rather than fixed high prices. About the only happy party in "price wars" is the consumer who is in essence a price-war profiteer: to him the lower the price, the better.

There is a need to understand that there are two kinds of monopolies: coercive and natural.

A natural monopoly is one which exists by virtue of the size of the market which it serves and the size of the company itself. A small-town general store that had no other competition could be called a natural monopoly, if the solitary existence of the store were the result of the population of the town which it served and not the fact that government had decreed that only one store should exist. In such a case, the store could be operating so efficiently that there would be no price margin that would allow another company to come into the town, charge lower prices, and make a profit. However, if the general store should suddenly raise its prices (either arbitrarily or to cover the cost of inefficient operation), then enough of a margin would be created to allow another company to come in and make a profit. So long as the store charged the lowest possible prices, while also covering its operating costs and operating at optimum efficiency, it would not be profitable for another company to enter the market.

Now suppose that the town was suddenly faced with a growth of population (say, a factory opened on the outskirts of town, attracting new families to the area). The general store could continue business as usual, leaving the market open for new competitors to fill the gap, or it could expand its business to accommodate the increased size of the market while hoping to maintain its efficiency and low costs. Of course, there is always the chance that a chain grocery will decide to set up a store in the town and may succeed in offering better services at a lower price with better facilities. This is the way things are on the market — things are constantly changing: new methods of production and marketing, new products, new tools, new knowledge.

Natural monopolies (unless they are very small, such as the general store in a one-horse town) are very rare and do not last long. This can be seen in the automobile field. At one time Ford Motor Company had a natural monopoly in low-priced mass produced cars. Then General Motors and

Chrysler and American Motors entered the game; other minor companies also came and went. During the last decade a large part of the domestic market has been taken over by imports. Although Ford is still a major auto maker, Americans can now choose from among dozens of competitive foreign and domestic companies.

The evils we commonly associate with monopolies are possible only when a *coercive* monopoly exists. A coercive monopoly, through the use of physical force or fraud, prevents competitors from entering the market. This can be done in two ways: through criminal acts, such as gang control of drugs, liquor (during Prohibition), or protection rackets: *or* through government sanction. It should be noted that both areas of action (criminal and governmental) result in a monopoly achieved by the use or threat of *force*; the difference is that in criminal action the means are regarded as wrong and cannot be performed openly, but in the case of government coercion, the force is sanctioned.

Therefore, since the use of force or fraud by individuals is considered criminal and is punishable by imprisonment, the only effective way that a coercive monopoly can be established out in the open is by government approval. The great railroad monopolies of the nineteenth century developed through government sanctions. The postal system has become a government monopoly. Most cities have only one transit system, which exists by virtue of a franchise granted to only one company. Other companies are restricted by law from entering into competition. Most cities have only one telephone company and other companies are not allowed to compete. Most cities have only one power company or water company and other companies are forbidden to compete with them. These are all coercive monopolies because they maintain their monopoly status in the market by virtue of force (the big gun of government). Furthermore, prices are regulated and, if service is bad, the consumer has no alternative but to keep dealing with the companies in question.

One of the best examples of coercive monopoly is the U.S. Postal Service. *No* one but the government is allowed to deliver first class mail (violations punishable by law), and no one but the government is allowed to put anything in your mailbox (even though you paid for it and it is your private property). With no competition, it shouldn't be surprising to find mail bags in railroad cars three years after they were placed there or important business accounts lost because of month-late delivery dates. Nor should it be shocking that despite rate increases of 100% or more in various categories, an airmail letter from Chicago to Miami takes an average of 58 hours to be delivered compared to the 23 hours it took in 1961. Twelve years ago an air mail letter from Chicago to Los Angeles took 19 hours to be delivered; today it takes 52 hours. Likewise, the 25 hours it took to deliver a letter from Chicago to San Francisco in 1961 has increased to 56 hours.[9]

But in third-class mail, government does not have a monopoly, and private profit-making services have sprung up, offering superior service and lower rates. The Independent Postal System of America (IPSA), created in 1968, recently offered to deliver one million Christmas cards for the U.S. Postal Service if they came to them at least 48 hours before Christmas, and they would deliver them at two-thirds of the price the Postal Service was charging. It would have been the first profit the postal services would have made in decades, but it was turned down.[10]

Also, in the delivery of parcels, private initiative is free to operate. The United Parcel Service, which now delivers more packages weighing over a pound than does the Postal Service, offers lower rates, better pick-up and faster deliveries. Although these were services in which the Postal Service claimed to be losing money and thus demanded government subsidy, UPS made a profit of $77.5 million in 1972, without government assistance.[11]

The Postal Service, although not paying property or Social Security taxes, still has a $1.7 billion deficit which is underwritten by the Treasury. Not only does the consumer pay higher prices because of the lack of competition, but the taxpayer also covers the cost of any deficits.[12]

We might also look at what has happened to the railroads. Government regulation has progressively stifled competition, and during the last few years the government has effectively taken over the passenger lines. The results: greatly increased fares, less personal service, shabby accommodations, and fewer rail lines.

AMTRAK, the government subsidized corporation which operates all passenger service crossing state lines, prints this on the back of tickets:

> Times shown on time tables or elsewhere and times quoted are not guaranteed, and form no part of this contract. Time schedules and equipment are subject to change without notice. Carrier may, without notice, substitute alternate means of transportation, and may alter or omit stopping places shown on ticket or timetable. Carrier assumes no responsibility for inconvenience, expenses or other loss, damage or delay resulting from error in schedules, delayed trains, failure to make connections, shortage of equipment or other operating deficiencies.[13]

In other words, you may not get where you want to go, and you may not get there on a train, and you may not stop where you thought you would stop, and the railroad is not responsible for inconvenience or injuries resulting from its own ineptitude. The only thing that you can be sure of when you ride the silver streak known as AMTRAK is that your chances are high that you will arrive on time. Why? Because AMTRAK has re-defined "on time." From the *Wall Street Journal* of March 14, 1974:

> In January, 1973, AMTRAK reported that 66.2% of its trains arrived on time. By December, 1973, the figure was down to 51%, so AMTRAK, a great fan of Newspeak, re-defined "on time." Under the old definition a train had to arrive within 5 minutes of the scheduled arrival time to be considered "on time." Under the new definition it may be up to a half hour late. Thus AMTRAK was able to announce an improved "on time" rating of 61.7% for January, 1974.[14]

You pay your money and you take your chances: this seems to be the way AMTRAK is run. If a privately-owned company, one subject to competition, were run like this, it would not be running long. Only with government sanction and with taxpayers forced to pick up the deficit, can a monopoly as inefficient and silly as AMTRAK continue to operate.

MINIMUM WAGE

The first minimum wage law (federal) was enacted in 1938 — the Fair Labor Standards Act. The principal motivation behind its passage was to encourage "the minimum standards of living necessary for health, efficiency and well-being of workers." It assumes, as does present similar legislation, that anyone who works has a legal claim against his employer, or against society, for a wage sufficient to assure an adequate standare of living.

When new minimum wage laws are enacted, the supporters congratulate themselves on opening the doors to higher living standards for everyone, particularly the poor. The rationalization takes the form of at least one of two justifications. First, if the employers were paying wages below the workers' productivity, i.e., "exploiting" them, then the law's passage would simply boost wages and cause no unemployment. Profits would be less and wages would consume a larger portion of the purchaser's dollar. Second, even if the employers were not "exploiting" their workers, the pressure to pay higher wages would force the employer into more efficient methods, thereby absorbing the higher wages without reducing employment.

But what are the actual economic results of enacting minimum wage laws? Henry Hazlitt in *Man Versus the Welfare State* writes:

It ought to be obvious that minimum wage laws hurt most the very people they are designed to "protect." When a law exists that no one is to be paid less than $64 for a 40-hour week, then no one whose services are not worth $64 a week to an employer will be employed at all. We cannot make a man worth a given amount by making it illegal for anyone to offer him less. We merely deprive him of the right to earn the amount that his abilities and opportunities would permit him to earn, while we deprive the community of the moderate services he is capable of rendering. In brief, for a low wage we substitute unemployment. . . .

The outstanding victim has been the Negro, and particularly the Negro teenager. In 1952, the unemployment rate among white teen-agers and non-white teenagers was the same — 9 per cent. But year by year, as the minimum wage has been jacked higher and higher, a disparity has grown and increased. In February of 1968, the unemployment rate among white teen-agers was 11.6 per cent, but among non-white teen-agers it has soared to 26.6 per cent. [15]

By July of 1973, *Business Week* reported:

Teen-agers are virtually frozen out of jobs now — unemployment of black youths in some cities may run as high as 40% — and the higher the minimum wage rises, the less economic it is to employ them.

Teen-agers now make up nearly one-fifth of the civilian work force. In 1972 there were nearly 16-million employable in the 16 to 19 age bracket.[16]

While the aim of a minimum wage law is to improve the incomes of the marginal workers, the actual effect is precisely the reverse — it is to render them unemployable at legal wage rates. The higher the minimum wage rate relative to free-market rates, the greater the resulting unemployment.

A simple economic principle is that goods or services priced higher than demand justifies will not find a buyer on the free market. This theory applies to potatoes, butter, milk, or an hour of a man's labor. If the seller, either by his whim or the government's, does not adjust his price in accordance with the demand, he faces "unemployment" for his potatoes, butter, milk, or labor.

Failure to allow a man to offer his services at the market rate deprives him of self-sufficiency and this is what minimum wage laws do. But, worse still, those productive powers are lost and our economy and society are poorer because of it. And who suffers most from these restraints on the available supply of services and goods? The poor — for whose benefit the law was passed in the first place.

There are reasons for some people earning

more than others: skilled labor should command a higher price than unskilled; a successful businessman should be paid more than any of his employees. But a compulsory minimum wage, whether set by government or labor unions, seeks to determine a man's worth irrespective of his productivity — humanistically admirable, but economically absurd!

LABOR UNIONS

Most people believe that, as a result of counterbalancing the enormous power of industrial manufacturers, labor unions are in large part responsible for a much improved standard of living.

It is commonly assumed that through collective bargaining these unions have improved the wages of everyone. For example, during the congressional inquiry into the 134-day longshoremen's strike in 1971, the President of the International Longshoremen's and Warehousemen's Union (ILWU), Harry Bridges, said, "My thinking is that winning this strike is the best thing for all workers." Although it might be a bit difficult for a department store clerk working for $2.00 an hour to see how he is gaining by a longshoreman's making $65 a day, it is still the basis of contemporary union philosophy that one union's successful strike benefits all workers.[17]

Henry Hazlitt, among other well known economists, contends that for more than a century economic thinking on this matter has been dominated by the "myth" that labor unions have been, on the whole, highly beneficient institutions. "The blunt truth is that labor unions cannot raise the real wages of all workers. . . . The actual policies that labor unions have systematically followed . . . have in fact reduced the real wages of the workers as a whole below what they would otherwise have been."[18]

When a union strikes for higher wages — higher than the market value of their work — the results of a successful strike, while appearing to gain higher wages for the members of the union, in many instances actually hurt them. Any gains union members receive from a strike are passed on to the consumers — to other workers (some of them union members) — in the form of higher prices. Thus, for example, while the longshoremen may have improved their positions (assuming the increases in their wages offset their not working for a third of a year, which is highly unlikely), everyone else was hurt. Bridges was able to halt all West Coast imports and exports for four and a half months with a strike that wreaked havoc on shippers, farmers, banks, common workers, and consumers alike. Even the longshoremen were hurt to the extent that consumer prices also rose for them. When these strikes are compounded we see that these union members do, in fact, gain something from their debilitating strikes.   But three-fourths of all workers are not in unions, and they are surely hurt by these strikes, for their wages are not raised at all and they, too, must pay higher consumer costs. If the constant demand for higher wages forces the producer to raise the price of his product beyond the market demand, he frequently has no choice but to go out of business — and that benefits no worker. So it simply is not true that strikes benefit all workers. They always hurt non-union workers, and many times they hurt even the strikers.

There are often other losses aside from higher prices and time off the job. During the last few years cities have suffered through paralyzing strikes of teachers, nurses, subway workers, taxi drivers, garbage collectors, fuel deliverers, oil-burner repairmen, grave diggers, newspaper workers, and others.

> The chief leverage of the strikers, in securing capitulation to their demands, was the amount of hardship and suffering they were able to inflict, not directly on the employers, but primarily on the public. Yet who are the public? They are in the main other workers, including other union members. They may even be members of the striking union itself and of their families. A striking fuel oil deliverer's own children, for example, may be sick and shivering because no fuel has been delivered.[19]

While union leaders and many politicians are vociferous in defense of labor's right to strike, they seem reluctant to admit that not all strikes are economically justifiable and, when they are not, these people seem to skirt the admission that for these strikes to be effective labor must find some means of preventing the hiring of workers to take their place. This "prevention" must be physical, if not violent.

In the building industry, for instance, the reported incidents against open-shop construction projects and employees cost $5 million annually. The reason for this problem is that many construction jobs are lost by union members because non-union contractors can outbid unionized firms on building costs. In many cases, this underbidding is possible *not* because of lower pay to the workers, but because on a union project each craft has jurisdiction over a particular field of work. Many times some craftsmen cannot proceed with their work until other craftsmen get to the project. Workers, although capable of doing the work, are forbidden to do so if they belong to a different craft.

In contrast, a non-union project director can move his qualified men into various types of work as needed without worrying about a certain craft's "jurisdiction." This maximum use of manpower is of great importance in operating efficiently.

June, 1974, marked the date when some unions began to realize this trend for themselves. The 25,000-member Operating Engineers Union

Local 12 disaffiliated itself from the rest of the building trade unions in the Southern California area. The reason was given by local head Joseph Seymour, "We might be able to get huge wage increases, and we would then have some beautiful pieces of paper to read in our homes while nonunion contractors take our jobs away from us."[20]

A reaction to the continuing expansion of open-shop contracting into the construction industry, a former union bastion, is union violence. It occurs usually in the form of physical attacks on non-union employees and building projects. The motivation behind this violence is the craftsman's fear of losing work. His union, in effect, has secured him wages above what a free market would permit. Instead of his skills being worth, say, $9.50 on the free market, they are worth only $5 an hour. And from the use of violence, it can be further inferred that others just as qualified as he are willing to work for a wage which by free market standards is fair and just.

Sometimes a company never has the opportunity to negotiate for a reasonable wage. In June, 1974, striking workers at a United States Borax and Chemical Corporation in Boron, California, burned down the personnel office, a guardhouse, a scale house, and a railroad boxcar. Then shots were fired at sheriff's department and company helicopters as they approached. Jim Boghosian, business agent for the union, Local

30 of the ILWU, said the situation was precipitated by the firm's attempt to move non-union workers onto the premises. "When the company opened the gates and brought in the scabs in pickups, this was too much for our men to take."[21]

Is this justification for the incident or just ordinary violence rationalized by the union's claim on jobs which its workers abandoned? The irony is that non-union workers were not being hired at all. The men coming into the plant were additional security guards.

One union which has succeeded in getting the public to sympathize with it is the AFL-CIO United Farm Workers. Yet, this union, led by Cesar Chavez (professed advocate of non-violence), has perpetrated acts of violence or threats of violence against not only the growers, but against their own ethnic and working kind.

> "I was warned by them [UFW] that I had better watch out if I was caught by myself if I reported for work."
> "They [UFW] said they would break our arms if we stayed in the field."
> "They [UFW] told me, 'If you don't get out of the fields, and if you keep on working, when you leave for home you'll pay for it.'"
> "They [UFW] said, 'If you go to work the Immigration will come and get you out of the field.'"

"I wanted to continue working, but I stopped because I was afraid."

"After hearing about being thrown out of the field and getting beat up, all of us on the crew stopped working."[22]

All of the above quotes are excerpts from duly sworn and notarized declarations by farm workers on file in the county clerk's office in Salinas, California. The reports of beatings and threats and general harassment continue through·out whatever strike or boycott the UFW undertakes. Despite overtones of "social reforms," much of the violence is common in a jurisdictional fight between two powerful unions — the Teamsters and the AFL-CIO. The results are that the farm workers are losing, the growers are losing, and currently it is a draw on jurisdiction.

How can everyone win?

In 1973 Cleveland's Lincoln Electric Company, the world's largest maker of arc-welding equipment, distributed over $21 million in "incentive bonuses" to its 2,200 employees. In all, since 1934 the company has given out over $200 million in bonuses. Although the basic wage is now $4.90 an hour, the bonuses, geared to reward everything from high productivity to low absenteeism, boost the pay to an average well over $10.00 an hour. The output and morale are so high that Lincoln has been able to sell its 300-ampere motor generator with only a slight increase over the 1934 price in spite of substantial increases in the prices of steel and copper. While the price has remained low over this 40-year period, the quality of the product has continually improved. Not even the cheap labor of foreign countries can meet the selling price that bonus-inspired productivity makes possible.[23]

Other industries have not been as fortunate. The counter-balances inherent in a free market economy have been eliminated by union domination and labor legislation. In a free market system workers would be paid according to productivity, but legislation has enabled unions to peg their demands according to their strength in their particular industry, and these demands are often inconsistent with the union members' productivity. The consequences are "featherbedding," resistance to new technology, and inferior production techniques. This inefficiency is passed on to the consumer through higher prices.

Unions are specifically exempted from the antitrust laws; thus, they can conspire to monopolize (and surely it is a monopoly to have only one union controlling all auto workers, one union controlling all metal workers, one union controlling all garment workers, and so on), but businesses cannot. Legislation passed to protect weak unions of four decades ago has resulted in monolithic, monopolistic unions which can get whatever they want for themselves at the expense of other workers and consumers.

The Norris-LaGuardia Act of 1932 greatly limited the power of the courts to issue injunctions against unions for prospective irreparable damages. In practical terms this means that a company has no way to stop union violence until after the violence occurs. Since illegal union activity can quickly bankrupt a company, under this law management is driven to give in to union demands in advance. This pressure to agree to union demands effectively does away with true bargaining (which is supposed to be a true give-and-take situation). This act also made unenforceable any contracts by which the employee agreed not to join a union, thus restricting the ability of the individual worker to voluntarily contract. A particular worker may have a better chance for a certain job if he agrees not to join, say, a union known for promoting violence on the picket lines; if he can not contract on this basis, the worker may very well be passed over for someone else.

Collective bargaining was made *compulsory* by the 1935 Wagner Act (National Labor Relations Act). If, in an election conducted by the National Labor Relations Board, a majority of the workers in a particular job classification (for instance, assembly line workers or maintenance men) choose to be represented by a certain union, that union is certified by the NLRB to be the exclusive bargaining agent for *all* the workers in that job classification. The company must thereafter bargain with that union. This act discourages employees from breaking away from one union to join another — the alternative union would not be recognized as having the ability to bargain, so why bother to join it? Although not all union activity comes under the Wagner Act, the powers of the NLRB under the Act are quite extensive; in fact, the NLRB is given wide authority to determine its own jurisdiction. What bargaining activity is not under the NLRB will often be found to be under the jurisdiction of state agencies with functions similar to NLRB.

The 1947 Taft-Hartley amendments to the Wagner Act outlawed the closed shop and the secondary boycott. They also sought to define "unfair" union practices. Twelve years later the Landrum-Griffin Act was passed. This statute prohibited a number of corrupt union procedures and undertook the hopeless task of clarifying what is and what is not a secondary boycott.

These laws not only violate the rights of employers, they also restrict the freedoms of workers. The federal acts assure union members the right to get their job back even if they go on strike. In other words, if a company hires another worker to fill the job vacated by the striker, when the strike is over the replacement worker must give up his job so that the striker can have his old job back (and there is no time limit in which the striker must make his job claim — it could be years later). With this system, it is just a matter of time until management succumbs to union demands. Furthermore, union members who do not want to strike must do so if the union votes for a strike. The law has severed voluntary relationships between the employer and employee.

If a company maintains labor camps as "self-contained communities," the company must allow labor organizers onto the property for purposes of unionization, as ordered by the Fifth District Court of Appeals.

If a company, upon discovering that a younger man is much more productive than an older employee of the company, fires the older man, he must be reinstated and compensated for loss of income.

If a union threatens to close down a company by not adjusting its demands, there is no indignation from the NLRB. But if a company sticks to its offer it is accused of "unfair labor practices" and "not bargaining in good faith."

In a free society workers could voluntarily associate themselves in a union, and workers who did not wish to join a union would not have to do so. Likewise, management in a free society would not have to bargain with any particular union; it would be free to bargain with a different union, or with several unions, or with individual workers. If union members were to strike, management would be able to replace striking workers with people who would be willing to work for the wages and benefits offered by management. Management might discover that replacing striking workers would be uneconomical, so it might encourage the strikers (who are already trained for the jobs) to return to work by granting part or all of their requests.

But these things are not really possible today. Modern labor legislation has so protected unions and has given them such power that for practical purposes there is no longer any true bargaining. A strike followed by a settlement is nowadays little more than a formal way of giving the union what it wants. This makes no sense, for the unions can't always be right, any more than companies can.*

PRICE CONTROLS

On the whole, the American public has not been aware of how the government contributes to artificial surpluses and artificial shortages of commodities through various price control programs. Nor has the public been conscious of the tremendous amount of its money that is spent

---

*For more information on labor legislation and union activity see Emerson Schmidt's *Union Power and The Public Interest* and Patrick Boarman's *Union Monopolies and Antitrust Restraints.*

on these interventions into the free market. All of these plans end up hurting the very people they were supposed to help.

For example, when the Great Depression first struck, the farmers were especially hard hit. The Hoover administration, in an effort to keep commodities stable, decided on a program to subsidize the farmers, hoping to keep the bottom from falling out of agriculture prices and saving the farmers from bankruptcy. The Grain Stabilization Corporation used $500 million to purchase surplus grain, but the sum was used up shortly and had failed to stabilize prices of the three major commodities in the program — wheat, cotton, and wool.[24]

The cost to the nation from this program was higher unemployment and wasted resources that came at a time we could not afford them. Despite this experience, the bureaucratic blunders were given a new lease on life by the Roosevelt administration, which decided the way to support farm prices was by controlling production. The Agricultural Adjustment Administration (AAA) was involved in many scandals, two of the more notorious being the slaughter of six million young pigs when a survey showed that in the near future prices would plummet because of large increases in supply; then the AAA required cotton farmers to plow under 11 million acres to support high cotton prices. Both actions sought to stabilize prices at a time when the average wage earner was receiving progressively less (if he were lucky enough to be working). The Supreme Court declared the AAA's actions unconstitutional, but undaunted, President Roosevelt created a new, more flexible AAA that again sought to keep food prices high, this time by reverting to the more accepted methods of price supports and government purchases of "surpluses."[25]

The point which simply was not understood (and still hasn't been) is that the government attempted to help by means of two self-defeating actions: First the government encouraged the farmer to over-produce by assuring him high government-controlled prices for his products and backing them up with subsidies and surplus buying schemes; then, alarmed with the resulting surplus, (at the artificially high prices, there was only a limited market), the government paid the farmer to destroy his excess produce. The consumer was the loser on both scores: He paid for the agricultural supports through his taxes, and then he paid the higher costs of the produce in order to eat.

The mistake of trying to keep prices artificially high during a depression should have been obvious, but it wasn't. As usual, a government program designed to help the poor did them more harm than good.

The same mistake works in reverse also: Today government wants to "help" in time of heavy inflation by (this time) keeping prices artificially low.

For example, price controls by the public utility commissions were a major factor in aggravating the shortage of natural gas. As the president of the 6,000-member Independent Petroleum Association of America warned back in 1965, the Federal Power Commission (FPC) "has resorted to a price fixing system that can only have the effect of forcing large numbers of producers out of the business of searching for much needed new supplies . . . Millions of gas consumers will, as a result, be the victims of the shortages of this essential fuel which are sure to follow."[26]

Decades of price controls have also discouraged development of alternate energy systems such as geothermal, tidal, wind, and solar. In Florida many homes employ solar water heating, but competition with price-controlled electricity and natural gas has prevented such technologies from being more widely developed.

Of course price controls cannot be blamed for the fact that the world's oil and gas supplies are gradually being consumed. This is a consequence of the industrial age. However, government intervention is a major cause of the failure of the economy to adjust to these changing conditions in a gradual and orderly manner.

There is a cardinal rule of economics concerning price controls: When the government sets a minimum price on a product and that price is higher than the free market price, an artificial surplus of the product results; when a government sets a maximum price on a product that is lower than the market price, an artificial shortage of that product results.

Private interests must take a share of the blame for the interventionist nightmare. But when the bureaucrat directs the economy, private interests will not hesitate to bend that direction to their own ends. The problems start, then, with government itself. Given the controlled economy, the rest will inevitably follow.

CHAPTER FOUR

KNEADING BREAD

In those areas most affecting individuals, the State has been equally adept at "turning every contingency into a resource for accumulating force in the government." The State has stuck its nose into moral affairs and has used these issues to broaden the base of its own power.

Particularly in the area of civil rights, welfare, and social security, the importance of individual freedom has been obscured under the guise of helping unfortunate people whose plight, in many instances, was most likely caused by government in the first place.

CIVIL RIGHTS

The Civil Rights Movement in the United States sprang up in response to the negation of individual rights — a negation that had its roots in enslavement of black individuals and the maltreatment of members of other minority races and ethnic groups. Thus racism was systematized and intensified by government intervention, and, the real issue — individual rights — has been obscured.

Government sanctioned slavery from the beginning. When 20 African slaves were first brought to the United States in 1619 to "help relieve Jamestown's labor shortage," they were eventually freed. Yet, years later the House of Burgesses enacted legislation that made all future slaves, slaves forever.[1] This practice became quite common in the United States. Because government itself recognized this practice as legal it became ingrained into the American way of life.

After the "Carpetbagger" era, Southern states enacted legislation guiding the activities of newly-freed black individuals. These state governments did everything possible to prohibit blacks from exercising their right to vote, primarily through registration requirements. In a spirit of "benign neglect," government played possum while the wolves of violence devoured the rights of individuals.

Civil rights properly refer to those rights which guarantee every citizen equal protection under the law and the right to participate in government to the same extent as every other individual. So long as the individual does not initiate force or fraud against another individual, he should be free to associate or not to associate with whomever he chooses — this is a fundamental right of all citizens in a free society.

Civil rights do *not* include, however, the right to violate the rights of others, for this is the negation of the very concept of rights itself. For example, in the Jim Crow Era, the government forced segregation. Now the government forces integration. Legislation which seeks forcibly to segregate or integrate private property should be opposed because both activities constitute a violation of the right of individuals to dispose of their property as they see fit. Since government in a free society must treat all citizens equally, the right to property applies equally to all individuals.

That is, the American love-it-or-leave-it patriot has rights, but so does the communist or the Nazi, so long as none of these individuals violates the rights of others through the initiation of force. Likewise, the American black has rights, but so does the white bigot — again, so long as neither of these individuals imposes his values on others by force. Men have rights but so do women — provided that neither violates the rights of another.

It is the role of government in a free society

to protect the rights of all its citizens, which it has undeniably failed to do in many instances. This should be corrected. But what has happened in many cases is that government has gone to the opposite extreme. Where it once refused to act on behalf of protecting citizens — namely, those who were subject to violence on the part of bigots — it now chooses to violate the rights of some people in order to grant privileges to those it previously failed to protect.

One example of such a violation of individual rights was cited in the April 4, 1972 issue of the *Los Angeles Times:*

> Two contractors who submitted the lowest bids on a $3,427,000 Los Angeles public works project were disqualified Monday because they failed to meet requirements of the federal contract compliance program for the hiring of minority workers.
>
> As a result, the city Board of Public Works in a precedent setting action awarded the contract to the third lowest bidder who attached an acceptable affirmative action plan to his offer. The difference between the rejected and accepted bids was $25,000.[2]

This action on the part of government was a costly one — both in terms of money (the bid accepted cost the people of Los Angeles — both black and white — $25,000 more for their public works than was necessary), and in terms of individual rights (the government rather than accepting the people who could do the best job for the least money, opted to accept those who had obviously set up a quota system among their employees — a system scorned for years by minorities because it worked *against* them). In this action the government encouraged discrimination according to race.

One of the latest proposed regulations of the Equal Employment Opportunity Commission deals with a racial census on college campuses. The Form, designated EEO-6, is designed for use by several federal agencies.

"White," say EEO-6 instructions, "should include persons of Indo-European descent, including Pakistani and East Indian." But it doesn't include Spaniards, or for that matter, anyone born in Latin America. They should be listed as "Spanish Surnamed." "Asian American," the instruction sheet adds, means not only "persons of Japanese, Chinese, Korean or Filipino descent," but also those "whose appearance reveal Oriental, Polynesian origins." "Other" is really a catch-all. It "should include Aleuts, Eskimos, Malayans, Thais and others."[3]

The problem of determining who goes in which slot is obvious and is aggravated by blunders such as leaving out many "races" which are in actuality Indo-European, i.e., Jews and Arabs.

Many others are not even covered by the proffered selections, i.e., Finns, Hungarians, Turks and Basques. Lastly, difficulties arose when a selection for American Indians had to be made. The solution? They are defined as "persons who identify themselves or are known as such by virtue of tribal association or consider themselves native Americans." In effect, being born in America doesn't make you a "native American."

The EEOC realized this fact, belatedly, and also provided a three-step plan to determine a person's nationality without asking (which is a no-no). As stated, "Eliciting information on the race or national origin of an employee by direct inquiry is not encouraged." Instead, the administrator can merely "look" at the person, providing a "visual survey." If that fails, he can categorize him by what "the community" considers him to be. As a *dernier ressort*, the subject may be regarded as in the group he "identifies with" — assuming, of course, that he selects no more than one "race-national origin category."

When race becomes the criterion of selection or the basis for action, then racial conflict is to be expected. Why not allow each individual to participate in a free market environment where each may act on his own behalf, operating according to his own values? On the free market color is not a significant issue. Legislation in this area is not only counter-productive, but in many cases leads to ridiculous regulations.

How does government interfere economically and cause race to become an issue more than it would have been otherwise? In his book *A Theory of Racial Harmony*, Alvin Rabushka explains it thus:

1. Governments take resources from the public but use them to maximize their own welfare. In the multiracial society this means the welfare of the controlling racial group, not the "common good" of all the citizens.

2. Government lacks the knowledge necessary for success (to achieve efficient allocation of public goods) because information is scarce and costly in the absence of markets. But in multiracial societies, government is not even interested in obtaining this knowledge; rather, government openly disregards the preferences of racial minorities and forcibly oppresses minorities by the use of its police power.

3. Administrative and policing costs often exceed the gains to be had from government intervention. In the multiracial society, political minorities bear the costs of administration and policing, receiving few or no benefits. Indeed, it is tragic that they are oppressed by the very group they finance.

4.   Distribution problems prevent efficient provision of public goods. In the multiracial society, rationing criteria are almost exclusively racial; public goods thus become the private preserve of the politically advantaged community.

5.   Government cannot devise an efficient benefit scheme of taxation. In the multiracial society, taxes are collected from members of all communities, but political minorities can be excluded from consuming all the public goods their funds pay for.

6.   Liberty is lost when government consumes private economic resources. Its loss is all the greater from the standpoint of racial minorities, who forego their private resources via taxation and are then later excluded from consuming public goods on racial grounds.[4]

Rabushka's conclusion? "Under conditions of voluntary exchange in free markets, racial tensions and conflict are kept to a minimum."

WELFARE

If a person robs you, we recognize that he has performed a wrongful act. But suppose some third party seizes your property in his behalf? Has the wrongful content of the act been altered? Suppose the third party is called a tax collector? Has the act of plunder suddenly become something noble and humanitarian?

When a government seizes your money in order to pay for programs that support others, how has its actions differed from that of a thief?

"But wait!" you protest. "This is different! The beneficiary of government welfare is in *need*!"

Need. Does this really alter the situation?

Suppose, for example, Mr. Jones is dying from a diseased kidney. The State seizes you against your will and removes your kidney for transplant. Did the State have the "right" to do it? Did Mr. Jones' need for a new kidney justify the State taking yours without your explicit permission?

Or, suppose a powerful country invades a weaker one for *lebensraum* ("living space"). It needs the territory for its growing population and for industrial expansion (so claimed Germany when it invaded Poland and Japan when it invaded China). Is the invading country justified in committing this action? Does it have a "right" to the land of another country because it is in need?

Or, suppose that you work for three straight summers in order to earn enough money to bicycle through Europe. The State seizes your savings in order to feed a needy family. Should it have the right to do that, because there is a need?

In each of the preceding cases, the need was quite genuine. The point is simply this: need does not establish the right to violate the rights of others.

It is true that poverty, in particular, has been a spectre haunting every civilization since man appeared on earth. It is also true that governments have a habit of instituting systems of relief for the poor, and the results are ultimately predictable: First, the programs invariably get out of hand and, second, poverty becomes greater rather than less.

Such is the case in the United States. As of October, 1973 there were 11 million individuals receiving Aid to Families with Dependent Children (AFDC).[5] This was an increase of 33% over 1970 when the figure was about 8.3 million recipients.[6] In New York City alone there were 328,000 welfare recipients in 1960.[7] In 1972 that number had grown to 1,275,000.[8] More than 10 per cent of the residents in the 20 largest cities in the U.S. are on welfare.[9] In the country as a whole, the number of people on welfare has grown from 6,052,000 in 1950 to 15,069,000 in 1972.[10] The number more than doubled in 22 years.

Government is notoriously inefficient when it comes to welfare programs. It is not rare at all to see up to two-thirds of the budget spent on administration while only one-third is available to the needy. For example, San Diego's program for Dependent Children of the Court during 1973 spent $944,532 for administration and only $322,384 on the actual support and care of these children.[11]

The infamous War on Poverty program is acknowledged almost universally to be an expensive failure. What then is the answer? Who will care for the truly needy? Those in genuine need are not just those who frittered away their money or who are "no good." There are many individuals who, through no fault of their own, *are* victims of genuine tragedy. Who will care for them? Will they simply be allowed to starve while the selfish individuals go about their own business with no concern for the welfare of others?

Consistently, individuals have voluntarily given great amounts of money and time to help those in need. In 1973, a year when the government was forcibly taking for its programs and administration about a quarter or more of each individual's income, these same individuals gave voluntarily over 24.5 *billion* dollars to charity (and 22 billion of those dollars were from individuals, not foundations or corporations).[12] It is interesting to speculate, on the basis of these facts, what individuals would do if they could spend their entire paycheck as they wished, rather than as the State forces them to.

To say that you ought to help those in need is one thing, but to say that you must is quite another, for it contradicts the very meaning of freedom.

There is virtually no difference in principle between forced collection of money to support welfare programs and involuntary servitude. In either case the individual is compelled by force to serve others.

In a free society the individual is not compelled to serve others. He is not compelled to give up the products of his life to the King or the Church or to the rich or to the poor. Whether or not one chooses voluntarily to help those in need is a question only the individual can answer. In a free society it is not the proper function of government to impose that decision by force.

When you honestly think about it, most people *enjoy* helping those in need. It gives them a feeling of satisfaction. And from this "selfish" motivation, those in need are most effectively helped. But when giving is mandatory, resentment is frequent. Many who previously sympathized with the destitute and the impoverished as innocent victims of "bad luck" become resentful and view welfare recipients as leeches or parasites. Likewise, many former recipients of private charity were grateful to those who helped them and made every effort to re-establish themselves as quickly as possible. But when giving becomes mandatory, many recipients begin to look upon their received charity as a "right" and demand more and more.

SOCIAL SECURITY

Social Security, despite current criticisms, is one of the best bargains ever offered to retiring people — that is, if you are planning to retire in the next couple of years. On the other hand, if you're just beginning to work, you probably will find yourself the victim of the most thorough fleecing since the sale of the Brooklyn Bridge.

A 65-year-old grandfather retired in 1973. If he and his employer have paid the maximum Social Security tax for the last 36 years, it would total $4,639.20. At the current payment plan of $317.24 a month, in 15 months he will regain all that was paid. At age 65 the average life expectancy is 14 more years, so he will gain almost 13 years of retirement benefits he didn't have to pay for. Social Security *can* be a bargain.[13]

Such a sanguine outlook may not be shared by his 25-year-old grandson who began making the maximum taxable wage ($13,200) in 1973. Depending on how you wish to play the game of statistics, either with or without inflation, the grandson's predicament can range from desperate to hopeless.

First, let's consider an inflation-wracked future. The 1972 escalator clause provides automatic benefits and tax increases if inflation exceeds 3% annually. Then the young worker and his employer will pay $85,000 each for a total contribution of $170,000 over 40 years. At a modest 5% interest, this money would become $370,000.[14]

The federal tables show anticipated monthly payments at that time to be $404.50 per month.[15] This works out to 76 years of payments. So, if the grandson lives to be 141, he has a fairly good deal. Or, figuring on the basis of 14 years of retirement (age 65 through 79), he would have to receive $2,200 a month to retrieve what he paid into the system.[16]

Secondly, let's say that there is no inflation for the next 40 years and the escalator does not apply. The grandson and his boss will have contributed $31,293.60, and with interest this will equal $73,275.00. Now, at current benefit rates, a man and his wife would both have to live to be 98 years old to collect what has been paid.[17]

Things are even worse if the grandson never marries or is a widower. His monthly payment of $218 would be less than his interest compounded at 4% annually. In other words, if the grandson lives forever, he could draw this amount indefinitely and never recover his equity. Even Methuselah would have been shortchanged by this plan.[18]

The 1935 introduction of Social Security legislation sought to insure the common worker that he would be taken care of in his declining years and that, if a family catastrophe occurred, his government-imposed "nest egg" would lessen the financial burden of disability or death. But, in effect, it is perhaps the most unjust tax ever legislated. Not only do the poor pay a higher percentage of their wages, but it is those in the higher tax brackets who reap most of the benefits.

The law states that 5.85% of your wages, up to $13,200 annually, is to be withheld for these "benefits."[19] The higher the wage goes, the less of a percentage of the wage is "contributed." Consequently, a person making $32,000 a year pays at the rate of 2%, while a $10,000-a-year man pays 5.85%. In fact, over half the families in the country now pay more in Social Security taxes than in income tax.[20]   And, unlike the graduated Federal Income tax, Social Security tax allows no exemptions. Many kinds of income are not taxable at all for Social Security purposes — capital gains, rent, interest, stock dividends.

Not only do the wealthy pay less percentage-wise, but they reap most of the benefits because they start work at a later age and generally live longer to collect payments. Conversely, blacks lose both ways, because they start work sooner and die earlier. Many who have paid into the Social Security "fund" will never receive any benefits because they didn't work the required quarters (totalling ten years) or because their spouses are receiving payments.

The notion that the boss is "paying his share" is a myth shared by legislators and employees alike. The employer's contribution is just another expense, like supplies or phone bills, and employee salaries are reduced by the amount that the employer "contributes" to Social Security.[21] That is, the money invested in Social Security is compensated for either by paying lower wages or by charging higher prices for goods — in the end, it is the employee as consumer who pays.

The major misconception about Social Security is that the system is an insurance fund to which people make "contributions" and later receive benefits or pensions. There isn't an insurance fund at all — just another tax to support welfare legislation.

This is true because Social Security was set up to be an actuarially sound government "insurance company" that by 1960 would be able, at any moment, to finance all the benefits promised to all subscribers. But, through increased legislation benefits and delayed tax hikes, the present trust fund has only $50 billion and is legally liable to pay over $500 billion in benefits.[22] This is a conservative figure. The *Wall Street Journal* reported in July 1974: "The most disheartening number, an official one, is provided by the Treasury Department. As of June 30, 1973, the unfunded liability of the system was $2.1 trillion.

Another way of putting it is this: In a very real economic sense, the national debt is at least $2.1 trillion larger than the politicians say it is. If, as of June 30, 1973, the system had refused to accept new workers, saying it would only collect taxes and pay benefits to those already covered, its outlays over the next 75 years would exceed receipts by $2.1 trillion, plus market rates of interest compounded annually. In the last year, this number has grown by about $300 billion."[23]

As one economist put it, "To call Social Security an insurance scheme requires a special skill in deforming the meaning of words in the English language."[24] If, in fact, Social Security was meant to be an insurance program, why didn't the government merely require that every person have old age insurance with a private company? Because the government thought it could do a better job than private companies. In effect, the Social Security system is just another piece of legislation by which government extends its power over the individual.

But the real trouble will come in the future. As Congress legislates more coverage and higher payment, it fails to realize that the burden on future generations to continue such support will be much higher than at present because of our country's tendency toward zero population growth. Fewer babies are being born, and better health care is enabling those who retire to live longer. This factor alone (forgetting for the moment the present trend toward earlier retirement which would aggravate the situation) results in an ever-increasing number of senior citizens to whom benefits will be paid; the work force will no longer grow, but the benefits and benefactors will. The consequence will be higher and higher tax rates to make up for the reduction in the working force. Just after World War II there were 20 workers for each Social Security recipient; today there are fewer than three workers for every one.

If the government didn't have a welfare program, people would be more inclined to provide protection for themselves.   If the government plan were competitive, people who wanted to join it would, and people who found they could get a better deal elsewhere would. If they failed to do either, then (just as in pre-welfare days) they could rely on private charity if the need arose. It's time to drop the "insurance" front and accept the system for what it is — a welfare bill doubling the size of the National Debt and destined to take an ever-increasing hunk of people's paychecks.

CHAPTER FIVE

BURNT TOAST

A dictator cannot stay in power without controlling the sources of wealth. Whether the "dictator" is one identifiable person or some abstract called the "State," the absolute necessity is control of the economy. In 1932 New Deal official Stuart Chase wrote:

Best of all, the new regime would have the clearest idea of what an economic system was for. The sixteen methods of becoming wealthy would be proscribed — by firing squad if necessary — ceasing to plague and disrupt the orderly processes of production and distribution. Money would no longer be an end, but would be thrust back where it belongs as a labor-saving means.

The whole vicious pecuniary complex would collapse as it has in Russia. Money making as a career would no more occur to a respectable young man than burglary, forgery, or embezzlement. "Everyone," says Keynes, "will work for the community and, if he does his duty, the community will uphold him. Money making and money accumulating cannot enter into the life calculations of a rational man in Russia. A society of which this is even partially true is a tremendous innovation."[1]

Now consider the comments of Max Eastman who, after devoting twenty dedicated years to the above concepts as applied in Russia, wrote his answer to all talk of planned economy in his book *Love and Revolution*:

I had believed, or hoped, that when people could no longer compete for private property [money], they would compete for honorific attainments [working for the betterment of society]. Merit, instead of money, would be the object of endeavor and the basis of invidious distinction. It did not occur to me that the new goal might be power — still less that the new rulers by getting power would manage to get most of the money as well. I had to learn also that power directly exercised can be more hostile to freedom, more ruthless, more evil in its effect upon the character of the wielder, than power wielded indirectly through a preponderance of wealth. . . . [2]

It would definitely seem that the best practical guarantee of political freedom is that economic system in which the sources of wealth are privately owned and controlled, rather than concentrated in the hands of the State. Further, the surest guarantee of political and personal freedom has been the free market — or what was almost a free market — and it currently appears that this guarantee will cease to exist in the years to come.

Today, the economy races along on the crest of the longest inflationary boom in the nation's history. And the safety valves inherent in a free market economy have been constricted more than ever before. Bankers need not exercise restraint because of concern for a general bank failure, because the federal government stands ready with its printing presses to prevent widespread bank failures from taking place. Spending will not decline, because the federal government will not let it decline. In short, the federal government with its elaborate system of "stabilizers" has, to an unprecedented degree, removed the restraints by which an unhealthy boom could be damped out before excessive damage has been done.

Does this mean that there will be another crash? Not necessarily. The boom-and-bust cycle is the distinct product of the "mixed" economy — the economy with sufficient government meddling to generate a boom, but still sufficiently free to "take the cure," to pull up short when things get out of hand. In the past, when conditions have finally indicated that restraint was in order, people have held back on spending and investing; now that option does not exist, for the major spender is the State. The present inflationary boom will not likely be followed by a brief, curative process of a depression, but rather by a very long period of slowly deepening stagnation.

Inflation, a gradual loss of freedom, ever tighter economic controls. Gradually, the effects are being felt. The economy is faltering, and the bureaucrat is calling for wider powers to cope with "emergencies" that never seem to end. It is becoming a hand-to-mouth economy. The industrial pace of the nation is slowing from a run to a walk, and from a walk to a crawl.

From a nation that has been taught that "the public interest takes precedence over individual rights," there is merely passive submission and . . . silence. There are too few who understand the simple logic of the French economist, Frederic Bastiat:

> See if the law takes from some persons what belongs to them and gives it to other persons to whom it does not belong. See if the law benefits one citizen at the expense of another by doing what the citizen himself cannot do without committing a crime. Then abolish this law without delay, for

it is not only an evil in itself, but it is also a fertile source for further evils because it invites reprisals. If such a law — which may be an isolated case — is not abolished immediately, it will spread, multiply, and develop into a system.[3]

Every great nation in history has collapsed ultimately into stagnation, decay, and tyranny. And it seems we are next. But is it inevitable?

PART THREE

People, asked from where it came,
Would very seldom know.
They would simply eat and ask
"Was not it always so?"

THE BREAD OF THE MATTER

What if government could not regulate prices or grades or qualities or penalize big companies or subsidize small companies? What if government could not regulate rates or terms or conditions, or punish efficiency or reward inefficiency? What if government could only use its power *defensively* to protect the life, liberty and property of its citizens against the initiation of force and fraud from others? What if the government could do nothing more?

What, in fact, would happen if the individual were free to buy, to sell, to trade, to produce, to rent, or to lease his property or service on any terms to which he could get someone else to agree voluntarily?

In short, what would happen if the government kept "hands off"? What would happen if the economy and the State were separate just like church and State?

Well, first of all, this economic system would be called laissez faire capitalism — an economic system in which all trade is based on voluntary exchange of goods or services, with government acting only to protect the participants from the use of force or fraud.

But secondly, and most importantly, there would be established the framework under which the maximum of individual freedom could be obtained. A free society.

Freedom is the ability to act without hindrance or restraint. When embodied in a political principle, freedom as applied to individuals living in a society refers to *the right to act or not to act according to one's own judgment, so long as one does not initiate force against anyone else attempting to implement the same freedom.* A society based on this concept of freedom has certain conditions which must be met before it can be implemented. A society based on this concept of freedom also has certain rewards to offer the individuals within it.

The question is: How important is this freedom to people (for only their desire for it can bring it into being), and are they willing to pay the price?

In order to give a rational answer to the question, it is necessary to have a basic understanding of the principles involved.

Principles are not legislated or invented — they are discovered. For centuries men were ignorant of the laws of physics, but they were subject to them nonetheless. It was only when principles were discovered that the great advances in the physical sciences could take place. So it is with human action. To the extent that the principles of human nature have been ignored or rejected, men have suffered poverty, stagnation, and political tyranny.

Because the basic principles of freedom are consistent with man's nature, they work. And because the basic principles of collectivism (statism) are not consistent with man's nature, they do not work, as not only history proves, but the state of the world today confirms.

One principle of freedom is individualism. It holds that the individual is justified in pursuing his own rational self-interest and, accordingly, he is not morally obligated to subordinate his freedom to the demands of the collective. The concept of individual rights is an expression of this premise. It means that one's life is one's own.

The principles of socialism, communism, and fascism are anti-individualistic. They deny that the individual has the right to live his own life as he chooses. They insist that the individual's primary obligation is to serve the collective, whether the collective be called "society" or "the State" or "the fatherland" or "the public interest."

Another principle of freedom is the right to fruits of your labor — property, whether the property be in the form of money, food, clothing, houses, boats, real estate, or whatever. Without the right to own and dispose of the products of his own life, the individual is dependent upon the State (or someone) for his very existence — his life, his liberty, and his property. Accordingly, if government is to serve men rather than rule them, it must protect private property rather than control it.

Under socialism, communism, and fascism, the institution of private property is not upheld. Perhaps ownership is nominally in private hands, but ultimate control is in the hands of the State.

The third principle of freedom is capitalism. When the institution of private property is upheld — when men are free to buy and sell and trade the products of their own lives free from interference — the economic system that results is capitalism.

Socialism, communism, and fascism are quite obviously not capitalistic. There are slight variations in degree, but the economic principle is one of interference and control. Wages, rates, profits and production are supervised by the

State, sometimes starting out quite insignificantly, but always progressing toward more rigid control.

Principles of political philosophy represent the criteria by which a political and social system can be evaluated. An understanding of the principles of freedom — individualism, private property, and capitalism — could have avoided the tyrannies of the past. An understanding of these principles can avoid tyranny in the future.

CHAPTER SIX

STAFF OF LIFE

It is late on the evening before your final exam in microbiology. It's been a very tough semester, but by burning the proverbial midnight oil you might be able to get out with your life.

Just as one scientific smudge is beginning to distinguish itself from another, there comes a knock on your door. Tearing yourself away from the fascination of cells and germs, you open the door only to be deluged by the tears of your neighbor. You sigh because you remember this scene from before.

Your neighbor has played an interesting role this semester. Although studying the same subjects as you, it is not with the same vigor. Instead, there is much more emphasis on "extracurricular activities." There is perhaps one of these interruptions each week with much the same outcome after each. And since your neighbor looks upon you as "so understanding and such a good listener," you usually get the call to man the tissue box.

What may have started as genuine sympathy at the beginning now borders on genuine contempt. This person has kept you from doing some important things during the course of the semester, and now the timing is really crucial.

The dilemma is what to do. You've probably made the decision already, but reconsider it from two points of view — the humanitarian (altruist) and the individualist.

The humanitarian/altruist has a deep, unselfish concern for the welfare of his fellow man. His actions do not consider himself, and in fact, some of them are detrimental to his own well being. But he is convinced he must not be selfish, and so he sits quietly listening to his neighbor because of his neighbor's need and his own unselfish determination. He will not think about the fact that he will surely fail the test in the morning.

On the other side of the issue, the individualist has little difficulty in making his decision. His prime concern is himself, so the neighbor is quickly shooed out of the room bringing the quiet necessary for study.

Many people, beguiled by what they feel is a

doctrine of humanitarian benevolence, think of themselves (or would like to think of themselves) as altruists. But the person who consistently practices altruism would regard it as a moral obligation to sacrifice at every opportunity, his happiness for others, his welfare for others, and ultimately his own life for others. People can preach altruism but they cannot live it. Nor should they, for the genuine altruist voluntarily enslaves himself to the need and desires of every other person. The genuine altruist — if there could really be such a thing — is not a man but a doormat.

The philosophical doctrine which recognizes the moral correctness of self-interest is individualism. It maintains that the individual is justified in pursuing his own self-interest and that, accordingly, he is not morally obligated to place the welfare of the group above his own. That such actions demonstrably result in a more productive and prosperous free society is merely a desirable consequence, not a principle.

Does this mean that the individualist rejects any sense of concern for others? Of course not. But it does mean that he recognizes as concerns only those relationships which he has voluntarily entered. Because he values human life he may assist those who are in genuine need, but the "obligation" is to his own values, not to the other person. The individualist does not regard it as an obligation to subordinate his own self-interest to the desires of others. And he would certainly resist any attempt to impose that alleged obligation upon him by force — nor would he attempt to impose it on others. What is important about this person is that he is not stringent, but flexible, and that he does not operate according to obligation or conceit, but by logical thought and reason and by self consideration.

It is quite true, of course, that individuals benefit from association with other individuals. One who lives the life of a hermit, removed from human association, must provide for himself and do without the company of others. One who lives in a voluntary association with others receives the benefits of the knowledge of others, the benefits of the production of others, and the benefit of the company of others.

But again, the real issue concerns the terms on which this association takes place. Is it voluntary or is it compulsory? Is it based on a mutual recognition of individual rights or the abrogation of them?

If all associations are voluntary, then the result is a free society in which each individual can make the most of his or her life. The only condition then is that no individual or group of individuals violate the rights of any other individual or group of individuals.

However, if men are compelled by law to serve the interests of others, it is not cooperation — it is slavery.

The Bill of Rights of the United States Constitution did not establish the sovereignty of "society," but the sovereignty of the individual. Neither did it require that the individual serve the State, the king, the nobility, the society, the rich, the poor, the public interest, the fatherland, or humanity. As long as the individual did not initiate force against others, he was to be free to live his own life without fear in accordance with his own convictions. It was individualism that was the basis of the most free and progressive nation on earth.

The philosophy of individualism grows out of a concept of rights, and this concept grows out of observing the basic nature of man as a human being.

For instance, if you were a hermit living in a clearing surrounded by impenetrable forests and never encountered any other human beings, the concept of individual rights would have no meaning. You would be responsible only to yourself. But when human beings live together it becomes evident that certain rules must be established to protect their lives, or to define how they may act in relation to other individuals.

However, on a purely social basis, it makes no difference if one believes that he has the right to his own life and is not obliged to blindly serve another or if one believes that sacrifice for others is a virtue. It is when one enters the political arena that the question of who is obliged to serve whom is no longer merely a matter for debate — it then becomes a question settled by legalized force.

By means of the coercive arm of the State, those opposed to individualism seek to impress upon the individual his obligation to others. The humanitarian seeks medical care for all — by force. He would encourage brotherhood — by force. *He would make men good — by force.* It is important to note that in a political system based on individual freedom a human being may practice any form of morality he wishes (including self-sacrifice) provided that he does not initiate force against others. But in a political system based on self-sacrifice the freedom to act upon one's beliefs is obliterated, because the humanitarian seeks to force his sense of "duty" upon everyone else — he employs force to make one human being sacrifice for another.

"To be a socialist," declared Nazi socialist Joseph Goebbels, "is to submit the I to the thou; socialism is sacrificing the individual to the whole."[1]

"We are going to take all of the money that we think is unnecessarily being spent and take it from the 'haves' and give it to the 'have-nots' that need it so much."[2] President Johnson.

Stalin: "True Bolshevik courage does not consist in placing one's individual will above the will of the Comintern. True courage consists in being strong enough to master and overcome one's self and subordinate one's will to the will of the collective, the will of the higher party body."[3]

"Ask not what your country can do for you — ask what you can do for your country."[4] President Kennedy.

Hitler: "It is thus necessary that the individual should finally come to realize that his own ego is of no importance in comparison with the existence of his nation . . . that the higher interests involved in the life of the whole must here set the limits and lay down the duties of the interests of the individual."[5]

But observe the contradiction in this argument. Humanitarians say that human beings must forget themselves in order that the "common good" can be served. But what is the "common good" but the sum of what is good for each individual that makes up a society? Therefore, how can the good of society be separated from the good of the individuals who compose it?

When each individual is allowed to live his life to its fullest extent without subjection to compulsion, then he is achieving the greatest good for himself. Since the initiation of force is not permitted in a free society, each individual is free to pursue his goals to the limit of his own capabilities. However, if the right of the individual to live in accordance with his own principles is prevented by State force, the individual's "good" is incalculably reduced. If the "good" for each individual is substantially reduced, then it follows that the "common good" is substantially reduced.

Americans have traditionally accepted both charity and self-interest as desirable components of human character, and have admired the person who demonstrates a balance of these two values in his actions.

However, a false notion has crept into our thinking that sacrifice of self is the "good" and individualism is the "bad." Therefore (so the thinking goes), since charity is desirable, it should be the philosophy of the land, and government should see that it is expanded. In view of this, it is not hard to understand how most people are misled into "buying" governmental humanitarianism. But advocating forced charity is like wanting cold steam or hot ice. Charity by definition must be a voluntary action. To force it is to pervert the character trait (voluntary good will) that prompts it. The results of forced charity will never be what people expect. Because humanitarianism is food for tyranny, this nation is moving steadily toward totalitarianism instead of a free society.

When Hitler shouted that it was the duty of the good German citizen to sacrifice for the fatherland, he would have shouted in vain were it not that too many "good" German citizens had been brought up to believe precisely that. As long as people choose to believe that virtue lies in service first to "society" or to the "common good" or to the "fatherland" or to the "public interest," there will continue to be dictators to see that virtue prevails.

It is by taking humanitarianism to its logical political consequence that dictatorships are established and the rights of individual people ravaged.

Controlled housing. Controlled prices. Controlled wages. Controlled business. Controlled unions. Controlled money. Controlled banking. Controlled television. Controlled news. *Controlled people.*

CHAPTER SEVEN

BETTER BREAD THAN DEAD

Private property has been the object of attack ever since the first non-producer enviously viewed the fruit of the labors of the first producer. The institution of private property has been condemned for perpetuating every manner of social injustice imaginable. Marx and Engels called for the abolition of it, and Pierre Joseph Proudhon, a social-theorist contemporary of Marx, declared, "property is theft."[1] But how can one steal if there is no concept of property? How can anything belong to everyone, or everything to no one?

For years there has been a long and tireless argument about property rights versus human rights. Yet even a small child could figure out that property has no "rights." Only *humans* have rights. However, the *rights* which humans have are "*property.*"

In an article entitled "What is Property?" William W. Bayes points out that the fundamental right for a human is the right to his own life. He *owns* his life. "His life does not belong to any other person or group. The *thing owned* is his body, and the related right to act, or property right, is the right to live. Now, matter is eternal, but human life is not; life must be sustained by procuring and consuming the means of subsistence. If we agree that man has a right to live, we must agree that man may use the mental and physical faculties to procure those means. Since the means (food, clothing, shelter, and the like) do not usually lie readily at hand, he must find or grow the food, manufacture the clothing and build the shelter. In short, he must produce."[2]

It then must follow that if production is necessary to life, and you own your life, then what you produce must belong to you, or there is no meaningful right to your own life. As Bayes points out, "a corollary of the right to produce is the right to keep that which one has created. If one may keep this product, it follows that one may consume it, exchange it for goods or services offered by someone else, sell it, or give it away. He may do all these things because *the right of the producer is anterior to that of any other per-*

son or group. [Emphasis added] To assert that he does not have a primary right is, in effect, to deny him any right whatever. It is to say that he holds his property by sufferance of anyone (including a government) who is stronger than he, and that it is proper to plunder. But if it is proper to plunder from the producer, then it must, *a fortiori*, be proper to plunder from one who has himself plundered. It must then follow that only might can make right — one may take from another when one has the might, and one may keep only what one has the might to defend. Unless a person is prepared to accept the 'might makes right' philosophy, he must respect another's right to live, to produce, and to consume, keep, exchange, sell, or give away that which he has produced."[3]

Property does not consist merely of real and personal possessions. Dr. Bayes continues, "Intangible, or incorporeal, rights which we Americans value as priceless, such as those guaranteed by the Constitution, being *things owned* and involving the *right to act*, are property. This means that such rights as the rights to free speech, to worship, to peaceful assembly, and to due process, are all property. If they are property, then the rights involved are essentially property rights. There is no right which is not property, and there is no property which, if not a right in itself, is not a fruit of the exercise of a right."[4]

That rights themselves are property is a legitimate part of our political heritage. John Locke asserted that we have property in our persons as well as in our possessions. Both Thomas Jefferson and James Madison believed that "government may not violate, directly or indirectly, 'the property which individuals have in their opinions, their religion, their persons and their faculties.'"[5]

At this point Bayes makes an observation: "It is interesting to note that many professors who do not share this traditional view of property pay it unwitting tribute when they insist upon 'academic freedom.' For so-called academic freedom is nothing more than the right to hold (i.e., to *own*) opinions and to utter (to *use* and *enjoy* and *dispose of*, as property) those opinions. If they are paid for a speech, an article in a periodical, or a book, they are being paid for the articulate expression of their expert (or perhaps merely interesting) opinion. It is absurd to suppose that they should receive payment for something that was not theirs to sell, not their property. The property lies in their opinion which is fortified and given commercial value by their expert background knowledge and their ability to express that opinion clearly and interestingly."[6]

The individual's right to do as he may wish with his own property does not include the right to do as he may wish with someone else's. The fact that an individual owns a baseball does not mean that he has the right to hurl it through someone else's window. This is not a limitation of property rights by "society" or by the State; it is merely the recognition of the equal property rights of other individuals.

For example, the abolition of slavery was not a limitation of property rights, as some would have us believe, for no such "right" existed in the first place. The institution of slavery was not an exercise of property rights, but a violation of them in that the slave was denied the right to control his own life. The abolition of slavery did not limit property rights; it affirmed them for all people of all colors.

In his history of the Plymouth colony, Governor Bradford describes how the Pilgrims farmed the land in common, with the produce going into a common storehouse. For two years the Pilgrims faithfully practiced communal ownership of the means of production. And for two years they not only nearly starved to death, but there was also great discontent with the system:

> For the yong-men that were most able and fitte for labour and service did repine that they should spend their time and streingth to worke for other mens wives and childre, with out any recompense. The strong, or man of parts, had no more in divission of victails and sloaths, than he that was weake and not able to doe a quarter the other could; this was thought injuestice . . . [7]

Governor Bradford wrote that "famine must still ensure the next year also, if not some way prevented." The "some way" decided upon was the introduction of the institution of private property, and the results were dramatic:

> By this time harvest was come, and instead of famine, now God gave them plentie . . . And in the effect of their perticular private planting was well seene, for all had, one way and the other, pretty well to bring the year aboute, and some of the abler sorte and more industrious had to spare, and sell to others, so as any generall wante or famine hath not been amongst them since to this day.[8]

The Virginia colony had similar experience. Captain John Smith wrote:

> When our people were fed out of the common store, and laboured jointly together, glad was he could slip from his labour, or slumber over his taske he cared not how, nay, the most honest among them would hardly take so much true paines in a weeke, as now for themselves they will doe in a day . . . [9]

Without property rights, no other rights can be secure. When property is controlled by the State, rights are not rights at all, since their exercise is conditional, depending ultimately upon

State approval. To argue to the contrary is to say that there are no rights — merely favors to be given to you or taken from you as determined by some one or some group.

In his book, *Fruits of Fascism*, Herbert L. Matthews quotes Mussolini as declaring: "Property is not only a right, but a duty. It is not an egoistic possession, but rather a possession which should be employed and developed in a human and social sense." And as Matthew observes:

> That, in Fascist terminology, came to mean that private property, like everything else, had to be placed at the service of the State, and one may well ask to what extent the institution (private property) was infringed upon by taxation, forced investments, and the whole structure of governmental interference which told a man what he should produce, how much, with what labor and at what price. In short, can there be a private property under a totalitarian system? Individuals are left with the title to their property, but since they can only use the property in certain ways specified by the regime, it becomes a form of state property as does everything else.[10]

To what extent private property is being placed at the service of the State in this nation today can best be contemplated on the basis of a few current examples.

In 1972 the voters of the State of California

passed by initiative the Coastal Zone Conservation Act which set up "Coastal Commissions" with almost unlimited, dictatorial powers. The Act defined the Coastal Zone as extending from the Oregon to the Mexican border, as far out to sea as the outer limit of the State jurisdiction and as far inland as the highest elevation of the nearest coastal mountain range. This tremendous area includes such cities as Los Angeles, San Francisco and San Diego. A portion of the initiative reads: *"The People of the State of California hereby find and declare that the California Coastal Zone is a distinct and valuable natural resource **belonging to all the People**."*[11] And if such preemption of millions of acres of private property were not enough, there is not one word in the language of the coastal initiative which refers to compensation for the expropriation of private property rights.

A former member of a California Regional Coastline Commission, M. Bruce Johnson, writes in *Reason* magazine:

> A land owner came before the Regional Coastal Commission on which I served and requested a permit to construct a condominium development on four acres on the California coast. The application was denied at a public hearing on the grounds that the erection of said buildings would obstruct the view of the water from the nearest State highway. The fact that a scenic drive already

existed between the water's edge and the parcel was dismissed as irrelevant.

Inasmuch as any structure — not just the proposed condominiums — would obstruct the view from the nearest State highway, I inquired whether there was *any* permissible use of the land. The Commission's staff responded that the four acre parcel might be used for a golf course or a cattle ranch. Ever played a round of golf on a one hole course? Or heard of a viable cattle ranch with four head of cattle?

Other projects have been blocked following staff recommendations for denial on the grounds that "the project would remove alternatives available to any agency in the area of planning." In other words, the right to use privately owned land belongs to the State, not the individual. The inescapable conclusion is that the owners of these parcels have been stripped of virtually all of their property rights without compensation. They retain only the title and the liability for taxes.[12]

Another example of this concentrated power concerned the proposed expansion of the San Diego Gas and Electric Company's atomic power plant at San Onofre. An official of the Atomic Energy Commission confirmed that the expansion plans were reviewed and approved by at least 33 federal, state and local (environmental and safety) agencies. It took San Diego Gas and Electric Company three years and almost $228 million in modification costs to receive approval from all of the necessary agencies. Yet on December 5, 1973, the Coastal Commission (which was voted into existence long after San Onofre's expansion was in the review stages) was able to veto the action of its Regional Commission and end the plans for expansion. Although the energy crisis and public opinion later caused these eleven men to reverse their ruling, the fact that they had the power to make such a ruling is inconsistent with the principles of a free country.[13]

Still another example of this Coastal Commission's power involved AVCO Community Developers, Inc., in Southern California. This large industrial conglomerate proposed to develop their coastal acreage with a combination of spacious condominiums (45% under county maximum density requirements), tennis courts, pools, public golf courses, etc. Beyond this, they made available to the county 34 acres of ocean front property for a public beach. The privately-owned land was completely graded for construction before the Coastal Commission was empowered. In order to proceed with construction, AVCO had to apply to the newly formed commission for the necessary permits. They were denied.

AVCO was then caught between the conflicting demands of two government agencies. On the one hand the county demanded that AVCO finish the promised public beach by a certain date, while on the other hand the Coastal Commission denied the required permits to complete the work. In the meantime, the company paid (and is paying) $15,000 a day in taxes on the unused land.

In an effort to save the rich top soil from erosion during the rainy season, AVCO proposed that the commission at least allow them to seed their own land with grass. This was also denied as it was feared by the commission that AVCO, as a result of having put more money into the development, would then have a stronger legal case. Two years have passed and the land, which is a vicious eyesore, continues to erode each rainy season until now, even during light rain, the ocean becomes brown from the washed-out soil.[14] Is this protecting the environment or the commission's power?

Without a doubt, many Americans, particularly urban dwellers, are becoming increasingly concerned about the social ills caused by over-development: traffic congestion, air and water pollution, urban sprawl, to mention but a few. But giving government more power to cope with these problems has not worked and government empowered to dispense favors usually ends up corrupt, inefficient, and dispensing these favors to those with "influence."

What are some possible answers to these problems? Adjust property taxes so a farmer's land won't have to be sold to developers in order to pay these taxes. Insure that property rights include the right to develop one's own land, but *not* the right to harm others by polluting the air, contaminating the water or causing an intolerable level of noise. Jeopardizing or causing harm to another's life or property would be illegal in a free society.

In effect, this is just what the Supreme Court declared in *West Virginia State Board of Education v. Barnette:* "One's right to life, liberty, and property . . . and other fundamental rights may not be submitted to a vote; they depend on the outcome of no elections."[15]

If this were not true, any legislation the majority could agree upon would be "legal," whether it would be forced sterilization for members of a particular race, euthanasia for everyone over the age of 65, or limiting the freedom of speech to those considered "responsible."

The initiative creating the California Coastal Commission and similar such proposals before Congress not only regulates a person's private property according to the vote of the majority, but there is no compensation for any damages incurred by the implementation of such regulations. The State controls your property. You just have the title.

CHAPTER EIGHT

BAKER'S DOZEN

The case for economic freedom does not rest entirely on its productive achievements: on its buildings, its houses, its automobiles, its bath-tubs, its medicines, its television sets, its sirloin steaks and green salads with Roquefort dressing. There is little, if any, evidence that man's search for purpose, his longing for fulfillment, is in any significant way furthered by these accomplishments. These accomplishments should not be scorned, nor should they be worshipped. Nor is there to be found in the lives of those who do worship them any evidence that they find ulti-mate peace and justification in their idols.*

*This and several other passages in this chapter are taken almost verbatim from "The Case for Economic Freedom" by Dr. Benjamin Rogge, *The Freeman*, September, 1963.

The case for economic freedom rests primarily on the consistency of the free market with man's essential nature, on the basic morality of its system of rewards and punishments, on the protection it gives to the integrity of the individual.

The free market may not produce the perfect world, but it can create an environment in which man may conduct his lifelong search for purpose in his own way; in which each day he may order his life according to his own vision of his destiny, suffering both the agony of his errors and the pleasure of his successes.

Total economic freedom would exist if the government's only function were to prevent the initiation of force or fraud against its people by any individual, group, or government.

Usually, when personal liberty is discussed, the concern is with man's non-economic freedoms — freedom of speech, of religion, of the press, of personal behavior.

Frequently, the most zealous guardians of these all important freedoms are outspoken advocates of eliminating freedom in the economic area. When it comes to commerce, to the making and marketing of goods, they are in favor of replacing freedom with rigid controls.

The question is: How long can these non-economic freedoms be preserved in a society that has denied man his economic freedom?

Freedom of the press, for example, is well-nigh impossible if the State owns the newsprint, ink, and printing presses; freedom of assembly is difficult if the State controls all meeting places and permits for their use. A free individual could not exist in a society in which the State controlled all means of employment and income, and hence the essentials of life: food, clothing, and shelter.

"Give me control over a man's economic actions, and hence over his means of survival, and except for a few occasional heroes, I'll promise to deliver to you men who think and write and behave as you want them to."[1]

In other words, when economic freedom is limited, personal freedoms ultimately diminish If this thesis is accepted, then there must always exist a tremendous presumption against each and every proposal for government limitation of economic freedom.

What is wrong with a state system of compulsory social security? It denies to the individual his freedom, his right to choose what he will do with his own resources. What is wrong with a government-enforced minimum wage? It denies to the employer and employee their individual freedom, their individual rights to enter into any voluntary relationship not involving force or fraud. What is wrong with government-to-government foreign aid? It denies to the individual his freedom to support only those causes he feels are justified. What is wrong with a tariff or an import quota? It denies to the individual consumer his right to buy what he wishes from whomever he wishes.

Strike from the books all legislation that denies economic freedom to any individual and at least three-fourths of all the activities now undertaken by government would be eliminated. It is breathtaking to think what this simple approach could do to the apparatus of State control at all levels of government.

Several months ago, a popular news magazine featured on its cover a cartoon of a shivering and bewildered Uncle Sam holding an empty Horn of Plenty. It is a fact, as Melvin D. Barger points out in his recent article in *The Freeman,* that the United States has been running out of lots of things in recent months. "There are growing shortages of energy, plastics, clothing, canned goods, paper, furniture — well, you name it. In 1973, without experiencing a major war or a disastrous farm failure, the long-time Land of Plenty was suddenly transformed into the Land of Not Enough. . . . There are, of course, a number of secondary causes behind our present shortages. But the primary cause of the trouble is that the United States has finally passed a major turning point in its journey toward socialism. The government's role in the economy has become as extensive and decisive that the country is beginning to experience the typical problems of other countries that have adopted socialism. Britain has had such troubles for years and continues to stagnate and to decline in world influence. It is not difficult to demonstrate that other countries have had similar difficulties under socialist governments."[2]

In the words of one historian, "The only thing we learn from history is that we never learn."

Socialism is not a new idea; in fact, many ancient governments attempted to implement it. In Sumeria (c. 2100 B.C.) the State owned most of the land and kept records of all business transactions. The Hammurabi law code (c. 1750 B.C.) fixed the wages of herdsmen and artisans, and established the price a physician could charge for operations. Egypt, under the Ptolemies (323 B.C. - 30 B.C.), owned the land and the mines; controlled banking; and regulated commerce. Nor was socialism confined to Europe and the Near East. China had several periods of socialism in which the government owned the land and exerted government control over commerce: Szuma Ch'ien (145 B.C.), Wu Ti (140 B.C. - 87 B.C.), Wand Mand (9 A.D. - 23 A.D.). Socialism was also an integral part of the Inca empire in Peru.[3] But one of the most famous and prophetic socialist eras began with the Roman Emperor Diocletian.

Diocletian, upon taking office in 282 A.D., proceeded to wage wars on encroaching Persians, Britains, and barbarians with brilliant success. His victories ensured Rome a generation of relative peace. But during these years of peace, economic decay set in.

To overcome depression and stave off revolution, Diocletian tried to replace the law of supply and demand with a controlled economy. To lower the unemployment rate he undertook extensive public works. Food was distributed to the poor at no charge or at half the market price. In order to insure steady supplies for the cities and his armies, he brought many areas of·industry, beginning with grain importation, under the State's control. In return for accepting this regulation, the shipowners, merchants, and crews in this trade were promised security in employment and profits. The State had long owned most of the quarries and now it prohibited the exportation of salt, iron, gold, wine, grain, or oil from Italy, and strictly restricted the importation of these articles.[4]

Establishments producing goods for the army, the bureaucracy, or the court were State-controlled. In munition factories, textile mills, and bakeries the government required minimum standards and purchased at its own price. Associations of manufacturers were made responsible for carrying out order specifications. If this proved inadequate, these factories were nationalized and manned with labor bound to the job. This went on until the majority of the industrial establishments and guilds in Italy were under government control. Government regulations controlled butchers, bakers, masons, builders, glass blowers, ironworkers, engravers, and so on. Historian Paul-Louis explained, "In every province special *procuratores* superintended industrial activities. In every large town the state had become a powerful employer . . . standing head and shoulders above the private industrialists who were in any case crushed by taxation."[5]

This system would not work without price controls so in 301 A.D. Diocletian declared maximum legal prices for all important articles and set wages for services in the Empire. This decree was an attack on those who were accused of profiteering from scarcity. The result?

> The Edict was until our time the most famous example of an attempt to replace economic laws by governmental decrees. Its failure was rapid and complete. Tradesmen concealed their commodities, scarcities became more acute than before, Diocletian himself was accused of conniving at a rise in prices, riots occurred, and the Edict had to be relaxed to restore production and distribution. . . .
> The weakness of this managed economy lay in its administrative cost. The required bureaucracy was so extensive that Lactantius, doubtless with political license, estimated it at half the population. . . . To support the bureaucracy, the court, the army, the building program, and the dole, taxation rose to unprecedented peaks of ubiquitous continuity. As the state had not yet discovered the plan of public borrowing to

conceal its wastefulness and postpone its reckoning, the cost of each year's operations had to be met from each year's revenue.[6]

Since the taxes were prohibitively high, everyone sought to evade them. A police force was set up to examine every man's property and income. Children, wives, and slaves were tortured to reveal hidden wealth or earnings. Severe penalties were enacted for evasion. As a result, the flight from taxes became almost epidemic in the Empire. Local aristocrats sought to escape election to municipal office, artisans deserted their trades, and peasant proprietors left their overtaxed holdings to become hired laborers. This situation progressed until, in the fourth century, thousands of citizens fled over the border and sought refuge among the barbarians.[7]

Many contemporary social welfare advocates see society as evolving from feudalism to capitalism to socialism. But according to history, socialism preceded the feudalism of the Middle Ages. The trend started by Diocletian was followed by his successors.

Perhaps the worst edict of them all was by Emperor Constantine. This 332 A.D. law bound tenants to their land until their "arrears of debt or tithes" were paid. When the landlord sold his property, the tenants were sold with it. Historian Will Durant states, "In this and other ways agriculture passed in the third century from slavery through freedom to serfdom, and entered the Middle Ages."[8]

This "social evolution" was not contained to just agriculture. Similar laws were established in other industries. The workmen were forbidden to pass from one shop to another without government approval, and no man could leave the guild in which he was enrolled. Membership in one guild or another was made compulsory on all persons engaged in commerce or industry. A son was required to follow the trade of his father. Whenever a workman requested a change in occupation he was reminded by the State that Italy was in a state of seige by barbarians and that every man must stay at his post.

These conditions were a direct outgrowth of Diocletian's decrees. Their effect was felt throughout the "Dark Ages" and was partially responsible for Middle Age serfdom. The European economy didn't recover from this period until such restraints on trade and other commerce began to be lifted during the fifteenth century. The subsequent Industrial Revolution launched the unprecedented era of productivity of the twentieth century. But this productivity may not last. "The only thing we learn from history" is that Diocletians never learn.

Scandinavia was at one time considered the perfect environment for the socialist state. Those countries — Sweden, Denmark, and Norway — already possessed many economic advantages:

abundant resources; a firm industrial base; and an industrious, intelligent, and homogeneous population. The result, however, has become the *reductio ad absurdum* of social welfare.

A prime example is Sweden. Although untouched by two world wars, it has failed in those areas of the economy in which it was expected to flourish. Serious housing shortages still exist. In the capital, Stockholm, and other major cities, people wait for years to obtain houses and apartments. Stockholm's rents, although under government control, are among the highest in Europe.[9]

Swedish hospitals are overcrowded and understaffed and admissions are often delayed for months. Doctors and nurses are in short supply. Homes for the retired and disabled are scarce.[10]

Although a larger number of students are attending secondary schools and universities, Sweden's educational standards have plummeted.

Early Swedish welfare advocates once predicted little crime when the basic needs of the people were fulfilled. But crime has increased more than 150% in the last 20 years, with violent crimes accounting for most of the rise. The number of robberies, for example, is seven times the level of the 50's. The police are able to solve only 30% of all crimes. Drug abuse and alcoholism are among the worst in Europe.[11] One Swedish official said, "Those among our political leaders who thought that serious crime and other antisocial excesses would be easy to control in a modern welfare state have been bitterly disappointed. It has become increasingly clear over the past ten years that the welfare state we live in is anything but an ideal society."[12]

A "strike mentality" has surfaced among both the blue-collar and white-collar workers. The country has been plagued by a series of legal and illegal strikes. Mines, railways, civil services, and schools have all been shut down at one time or another.

In a country where the government guarantees full employment, the unemployment rate has jumped to 3.6%.[13]

In a country which expects little or no inflation, prices are rising 11% annually.[14]

And footing the bill is the taxpayer. Roughly 42 cents out of every dollar of the gross national product goes to the tax collector to finance welfare state benefits.[15] A couple earning $6,000 pays 32% in income taxes alone.[16] A family earning $10,000 pays 40%.[17] For every dollar a Swede earns above $12,000 a year, 70 cents goes to the tax collector.[18] Indirect taxes add to the total: sales tax is 17.6% on all goods and services.[19]

The situation is similar in Denmark. The ordinary worker pays about 50% of his final earnings in income tax in addition to 15% sales tax on everything he buys. Inflation has been getting worse and is now at 14% a year. The slums still persist in Copenhagen. The per capita expenditures for social services have more than tripled in the past decade.[20]

As a result all the Scandinavian countries are experiencing, to some degree, a taxpayers' revolt. Socialist parties, which have controlled these countries since the 1930's, are finding themselves challenged on an unprecedented scale. An ex-cabinet minister described the situation in one word: "disillusionment."[21]

Challenging the established parties in Denmark is an eight-month-old taxpayers' party which advocates the eilimination of income tax and the firing of 90% of all public administration personnel. According to a poll taken in July of 1974, this party ranked third in public popularity and second in parliamentary power.[22] The architects of Scandinavia's socialism have been suddenly thrown on the defensive and are predicting a period in which public services will not be expanded, and may in fact, be curtailed.

During the post-war era, Sri Lanka (formerly known as Ceylon) came to be known as the "Sweden of Asia." This lush island paradise, virtually the only country in Asia without famine, class struggles, or industrial underdevelopment, has been the showplace of socialist reformers. The inhabitants of this small nation had had, under a series of colonial rulers, an efficient agricultural system, a high level of educational attainment, and little civil strife. But using the most advanced theories of government intervention, the socialist reformers have managed, in scarcely more than a quarter of a century, to destroy the economy, to encourage violent uprisings, and to place in power a regime with almost totalitarian powers.

Shops have little to sell and, as the quality of goods deteriorates, there is less worth buying. Tailors buy their thread on the black market. It takes four doses of expensive local antibiotic to equal one normal dose from the West. The matches are considered the world's worst, but they are needed in case of frequent power blackouts. During certain hours of the day no fresh water is available in Colombo, the capital, because the waterworks machinery is decrepit and cannot be replaced for lack of foreign currency.[23]

The cause of all the trouble is the widening gap between income and expenditure, the result of inefficient tax schemes, and extravagant social welfare programs. The economy reels under a 260 million dollar burden of food subsidies and free services for the entire population, an amount equal to half the country's annual revenue. The government pays for everything from education and medical care to bus service. The most regressive tax measure is the $200-per-month ceiling on expendable individual income. It encourages highly skilled workers to emigrate and undermines the initiative of those who remain. The Business Acquisitions Act allows the government to take over any commercial concern, and so the economy has been put in limbo. Double book-keeping is a common practice, for without it many businesses would not survive. Savings are likely to be in gems (the true hard currency) and smuggling is rampant and routine.[24] Out of a total population of 13 million, one million are unemployed.[25]

Each successive government promises more and delivers even less. In 1970 Mrs. Sirimavo Bandaranaike became Prime Minister, promising the masses more free rice than ever before. With the country 30% short of self-sufficiency in rice, and its production in decline (down by 15% in 1973), the government doled out a free kilo weekly for each person, and for most people it subsidizes a second portion.[26] With the politics of rice, the government is apparently working against itself. Since the producers are subsidized by the government, any increase in productivity would place a corresponding burden on the budget. If anything, the dole and the accompanying rhetoric have raised expectations to an unrealistic level. To fulfill them would mean total economic collapse, and to disappoint them would be political suicide.

Mrs. Bandaranaike's economic policies have brought with them an increase in political tensions. In April, 1971, about a thousand youths launched an insurgency that has been described as "more folly than rebellion." They were easily and brutally crushed. It is not a subject discussed in Sri Lanka, but the *London Sunday Times* estimated that there were 5,000 deaths and 16,000 detentions.[27]

The most effective opposition to the government comes from the press (seventeen dailies — five in English). The government recently passed the Press Council Act, which sets up a seven-member council to punish publishers and individual journalists for "untrue, distorted, or improper reports" with fines of up to $800 and jail sentences of up to two years. The Minister of Justice, the author of the bill, reports that the government is also planning to enforce "collective state ownership" of all major newspaper groups before the 1977 elections.[28]

Early in 1974, Mrs. Bandaranaike, pressed by talk of attempts to overthrow her government, imposed a state of emergency. Using her powers with special force, she took control of the biggest newspaper combine, closed down the country's second-biggest newspaper group, and seized control of the country's radio[29] for being critical of her leftist policies. The most controversial of her policies, as always, involved food supplies. Although her government won by a landslide in the 1970 election, largely by promising to boost the weekly free rice ration, it has since been forced to cut and vary the amount. The distribution of a basic minimum of free rice has become a way of life in Sri Lanka, and governments have been routinely tipped out of office for tampering with them.

But there seems to be little evidence that the repeated failures of socialism have had any effect upon those advocating more and more socialism for the United States. "If anything," says Melvin Barger, "the failures of socialist interventionism seem to provide the basis for new rounds of interventions. The delusion still persists that Government can solve our economic and social problems by appointing a 'czar' to supervise an ailing industry or by providing funds to support a certain cause. It is still not seen that the effect of this intervention must be to lower output and to inhibit the very market forces that can bring efficiency and order into our economic affairs.... The price we must pay, in this new world of socialist intervention, is very high in terms of lost liberty and lowered productivity."[30]

It is true that anyone can argue (and many do) the relativity of freedom. It must be granted that to some freedom of speech, religion, and the press are not as important as knowing that as many people as possible will be fed, clothed, and housed. But having as many people fed, clothed, and housed as possible is *absolutely* dependent upon production. How can Sri Lanka give rice to everyone, if there isn't any rice to give?

Why should the rice grower in Sri Lanka work to produce an excess when he can get his rice free? Why should he be expected to place more effort into production of rice than he will get out of it? Likewise, once he discovers that he will get his rice whether or not he works, why should he work at all? Then, as one by one the rice growers in Sri Lanka see no purpose to their continued efforts, where will the rice come from? It becomes evident that "no one gets it if there isn't any."

Not only is production diminished when the State determines the allocation of excess yield. Personal freedoms also diminish. When the right to economic freedom is taken away, it is not long before it is necessary to subdue non-economic freedoms as well. It is no mere coincidence that Sri Lanka's government now finds it necessary to control the press, that dissenters in Red China find themselves in a special school contemplating the virtues of Mao, or that Aleksandr Solzhenitsyn is expelled from the writers' union and prevented from publishing his works in the U.S.S.R. Economic shackles and the loss of non-economic freedoms seem to go hand in hand in collectivist societies.

"The inherent danger of socialism is that in establishing a social machinery for economic direction it creates a concentration of power — the coercive power of the State and the power of a focused economy — far beyond anything capitalism dreamed of and makes men far more dependent than free."[31]

This does not mean that capitalism is an elixir guaranteed to solve all of the problems which confront mankind. Capitalism will not provide human beings with happiness, if they do not know what will make them happy; it will not guarantee justice, if they do not know why justice is necessary; it will not protect them from the throes of materialism, if they wish to place products before people. These things fall within the scope of individual prerogative. What capitalism will do is provide human beings with the material means of survival and the freedom to improve their lives in accordance with their own wishes.

Probably very few people prefer government control over their actions and lives, but lately, not very many people have been able to see that a middle-of-the-road policy toward collectivism doesn't lead to more freedom or security for the individual. It only leads to less — and less — and less.

And somewhere Tom Smith is . . . laughing.

PART FOUR

TOM SMITH
AND HIS INCREDIBLE BREAD MACHINE

TOM SMITH
AND HIS INCREDIBLE BREAD MACHINE

by R.W. Grant

This is a legend of success and plunder
And a man, Tom Smith, who squelched world
      hunger.
Now, Smith, an inventor, had specialized
In toys. So, people were surprised
When they found that he instead
Of making toys, was BAKING BREAD!

The way to make bread he'd conceived
Cost less than people could believe.
And not just make it! This device
Could, in addition, wrap and slice!
The price per loaf, one loaf or many:
The miniscule sum of under a penny.

Can you imagine what this meant?
Can you comprehend the consequent?
The first time yet the world well fed!
And all because of Tom Smith's bread.

A citation from the President
For Smith's amazing bread.
This and other honors too
Were heaped upon his head.

But isn't it a wondrous thing
How quickly fame is flown?
Smith, the hero of today —
Tomorrow, scarcely known.

Yes, the fickle years passed by;
Smith was a millionaire,
But Smith himself was now forgot —
Though bread was everywhere.
People, asked from where it came,
Would very seldom know.
They would simply eat and ask,
"Was not it always so?"

However, Smith cared not a bit,
For millions ate his bread,
And "Everything is fine," thought he,
"I am rich and they are fed!"

Everything was fine, he thought?
He reckoned not with fate.

Note the sequence of events
Starting on the date
On which the business tax went up.
Then, to a slight extent,
The price on every loaf rose too:
Up to one full cent!

"What's going on?" the public cried,
"He's guilty of pure plunder.
He has no right to get so rich
On other people's hunger!"

(A prize cartoon depicted Smith
With fat and drooping jowls
Snatching bread from hungry babes
Indifferent to their howls!)

Well, since the Public does come first,
It could not be denied
That in matters such as this,
The Public must decide.
So, antitrust now took a hand.
Of course, it was appalled
At what it found was going on.
The "bread trust," it was called.

Now this was getting serious.
So Smith felt that he must
Have a friendly interview
With the men in antitrust.
So, hat in hand, he went to them.

They'd surely been misled;
No rule of law had he defied.
But then their lawyer said:

"The rule of law, in complex times,
Has proved itself deficient.
We much prefer the rule of men!
It's vastly more efficient.
Now, let me state the present rules,"
The lawyer then went on,
"These very simple guidelines
You can rely upon:
You're gouging on your prices if
You charge more than the rest.
But it's unfair competition
If you think you can charge less.

"A second point that we would make
To help avoid confusion:
Don't try to charge the same amount:
That would be collusion!
You must compete. But not too much,
For if you do, you see,
Then the market would be yours —
And that's monopoly!"

Price too high? Or price too low?
Now, which charge did they make?
Well, they weren't loath to charging both
With Public Good at stake!

In fact, they went one better —
They charged "monopoly!"
No muss, no fuss, oh woe is us,
Egad, they charged all three!

"Five years in jail," the judge then said.
"You're lucky it's not worse.
Robber Barons must be taught
Society Comes First!"

Now, bread is baked by government.
And as might be expected,
Everything is well controlled;
The public well protected.

True, loaves cost a dollar each.
But our leaders do their best.
The selling price is half a cent.
(Taxes pay the rest!)

FOOTNOTES

NOTES TO "WHEAT FROM CHAFF"

1 Internal Revenue Service News Release No. IR-380, May 15, 1961.
2 *Los Angeles Times*, April 4, 1965.
3 Ibid., February 27, 1974.
4 Ibid., December 4, 1973.

NOTES TO "THE BREAD ALSO RISES" (CHAPTER ONE)

1 Clarence B. Carson, *Throttling the Railroads* (New York: The Foundation for Economic Education, 1971), p. 23.
2 Ibid., p. 32.
3 Matthew Josephson, *The Robber Barons* (New York: Harcourt, Brace and World, 1934), p. 78.
4 Ibid., p. 165.
5 Ibid., pp. 18-19, 66.
6 Ibid., p. 236.
7 *New York Times*, August 27, 1961.
8 Clarence B. Carson, op. cit., pp. 53-54.
9 Ibid.
10 Benjamin A. Rogge, "Will Capitalism Survive?," *Imprimis* (Vol. 3, No. 5), May, 1974, p. 3.
11 Gabriel Kolko, *The Triumph of Conservatism* (Chicago: Quadrangle Books, 1963), pp. 57-58.
12 Clarence B. Carson, op. cit., p. 47.
13 W.H. Hutt, "The Factory System of the Early Nineteenth Century," in F.A. Hayek, *Capitalism and the Historians* (Chicago: University of Chicago Press, 1954), p. 176.
14 Ibid., T.S. Ashton, "Treatment of Capitalism by Historians," pp. 50-51.
15 Friedrich Engles, *The Condition of the Working Class in England in 1844* (London: George Allen and Unwin, 1892), p. 170.
16 J.L. and Barbara Hammond, *Lord Shaftesbury* (London: Constable, 1933), p. 16.
17 B.L. and A. Harrison, *A History of Factory Legislation* (New York: Augustus M. Kelly, 1966), p. 34.

NOTES TO "THE SUN SINKS IN THE YEAST"
(CHAPTER TWO)

1   Murray N. Rothbard, *America's Great Depression* (Los Angeles: Nash Publishing, 1972), p. 88.
2   *The Federal Reserve System, Purposes and Functions, Fiftieth Anniversary Edition* (Washington D.C.: Board of Governors of the Federal Reserve System, 1963), pp. 69, 75.
3   Murray N. Rothbard, op. cit., p. 113.
4   Ibid., p. 129.
5   Benjamin M. Anderson, *Economics and the Public Welfare* (New York: D. van Nostrand, 1949), pp. 182-83.
6   Samuel Eliot Morison, *The Oxford History of The American People* (New York: Oxford University Press, 1965), p. 942.
7   Benjamin M. Anderson, op. cit., p. 488.
8   Murray N. Rothbard, op. cit., pp. 203-05.
9   Ibid., p. 206.
10 Benjamin M. Anderson, op. cit., p. 222.
11 Ibid., p. 488.
12 Ibid.
13 Mary Bennett Peterson, *The Regulated Consumer* (Los Angeles: Nash Publishing, 1971), p. 79.
14 Clarence H. Cramer, *American Enterprise Free and Not So Free* (Boston: Little, Brown and Company, 1972), p. 220.
15 Benjamin M. Anderson, op. cit., p. 317.
16 Ibid., p. 319.
17 Ibid., pp. 348-49.
18 Ibid.
19 "The Morgenthau Diaries," *Colliers*, October 25, 1947.
20 Garet Garrett, *The People's Pottage* (Caldwell: Caxton Printers, 1958), p. 36.
21 Ibid., p. 37.
22 Benjamin M. Anderson, op. cit., p. 335.
23 Ibid., p. 338.
24 Schecter v. U.S. 295 U.S. 495 (1935).
25 John Maynard Keynes, "National Self-Sufficiency," *The Yale Review*, Summer 1933, pp. 760-61.
26 Murray N. Rothbard, op. cit., p. 295.

NOTES TO "THE NO-DOUGH POLICY"
(CHAPTER THREE)

1 Cf., *The Economic Development of Kuwait* (Baltimore: John Hopkins Press, 1965); Ragaei El Mallakh, *Economic Development and Regional Cooperation: Kuwait* (Chicago: The University of Chicago Press, 1968).

2 "Playboy Interview: Milton Friedman," *Playboy Magazine*, February, 1973.

3 Lawrence Fertig, "Right Premise – Wrong Conclusion," *The Freeman*, January, 1967, p. 17.

4 Ibid., pp. 14-15.

5 Harold Fleming, *Ten Thousand Commandments* (New York: The Foundation For Economic Education, 1951), p. 20.

6 Ibid., p. 55.

7 Firestone Tire and Rubber Company, *1973 Annual Report*, p. 3.

8 Cf., Adam Smith, *An Inquiry Into The Nature And Causes Of The Wealth Of Nations* (New Rochelle: Arlington House, 1966).

9 *U.S. News & World Report*, March 19, 1973.

10 Rick Weyna, "Private Mail Service: Free Enterprise At Work," *The Alternative Educational News Service*, December 6, 1971, pp. 1-2.

11 *U.S. News & World Report*, September 10, 1973.

12 Ibid., March 19, 1973.

13 "Conditions of Contract" on AMTRAK Passenger Ticket, Form 04.

14 *Wall Street Journal*, March 14, 1974.

15 Henry Hazlitt, *Man vs. The Welfare State* (New Rochelle: Arlington House, 1970), pp. 23-25.

16 *Business Week*, July, 1973.

17 Emerson P. Schmidt, *Union Power And The Public Interest* (Los Angeles: Nash Publishing, 1973), p. 78.

18 Henry Hazlitt, *The Conquest of Poverty* (New Rochelle: Arlington House, 1973), p. 131.

19 Ibid., p. 136.

20 *Los Angeles Times*, June 21, 1974.

21 Ibid., June 16, 1974.

22 See sworn statements on file: Monterey County, California,

Superior Court, Sheriff's Department, Highway Patrol; Salinas City Police, Hospital Emergency Room records — Aug./ Sept./Oct., 1970, Salinas, Monterey County, California. See also the pamphlet prepared by the Citizens Committee for Agriculture, 329 Pajoro Street, Salinas, California, September 13, 1970.

23 Letter: Mr. Richard S. Sabo, The Lincoln Electric Company, July 5, 1974.

24 Roger LeRoy Miller, "The Helping Hand Behind Food Prices," *Harper's Magazine*, February, 1974, p. 16.

25 Ibid., pp. 14-15.

26 *Wall Street Journal*, August 6, 1965.

NOTES TO "KNEADING BREAD"
(CHAPTER FOUR)

1   William L. Katz, *Eyewitness: The Negro in American History* (New York: Pitman Publishing, 1967), p. 20.

2   *Los Angeles Times*, April 4, 1972.

3   *Wall Street Journal*, May 29, 1974.

4   Alvin Rabushka, *A Theory Of Racial Harmony* (Columbia: University of South Carolina Press, 1974), pp. 93-94.

5   *U.S. News & World Report*, October 1, 1973.

6   Henry Hazlitt, *The Conquest of Poverty* (New Rochelle: Arlington House, 1973), p. 102.

7   Ibid., p. 93.

8   Ibid.

9   Ibid.

10 Ibid., p. 94.

11 C. Tudor, editor, *The Prolific Government* (San Diego: World Research, 1973), pp. 126-27.

12 *U.S. News & World Report*, April 8, 1974.

13 *Youth and the 1972 Social Security Act* (San Mateo: National Federation of Independent Business, 1974), p. 1.

14 Ibid., p. 3.

15 Ibid.

16 Ibid.

17 National Federation of Independent Business News Release, April 8, 1974, p. 1.

18 Ibid., p. 4.

19 Roger LeRoy Miller, "Social Security: The Cruelest Tax," *Harper's Magazine*, June 1974, p. 22.
20 Ibid.
21 Ibid.
22 Ibid., p. 23.
23 *Wall Street Journal*, July 15, 1974.
24 Roger LeRoy Miller, op. cit., p. 24.

NOTES TO "BURNT TOAST"
(CHAPTER FIVE)

1 Stuart Chase, *A New Deal* (New York: MacMillan, 1932), p. 163.
2 Max Eastman, *Love and Revolution* (New York: Random House, 1964), p. 633.
3 Frederic Bastiat, *The Law* (New York: The Foundation For Economic Education, 1962), p. 62.

NOTES TO "STAFF OF LIFE"
(CHAPTER SIX)

1 Arthur M. Schlesinger, *The Vital Center* (New York: Houghton-Mifflin, 1962), p. 54.
2 *Los Angeles Times*, March 3, 1965.
3 Arthur M. Schlesinger, op. cit., p. 56.
4 Milton Friedman, *Capitalism and Freedom* (Chicago: The University of Chicago Press, 1962), p. 2.
5 Cited by Ayn Rand, *The Fascist New Frontier* (New York: National Branden Institute, 1963), p. 4.

NOTES TO "BETTER BREAD THAN DEAD"
(CHAPTER SEVEN)

1 Cited by William W. Bayes, "What Is Property?," *The Freeman*, July, 1970, p. 392.
2 Ibid., pp. 394-95.
3 Ibid., pp. 395-96.
4 Ibid., p. 397.
5 Ibid.
6 Ibid., 397-98.

7 Henry Hazlitt in *Cliches of Socialism* (New York: The Foundation For Economic Education, 1962), pp. 174-75.
8 Ibid.
9 Ibid.
10 Herbert L. Matthews, *Fruits of Fascism* (New York: Harcourt, Brace and World, 1943), pp. 144-45.
11 M. Bruce Johnson, "Piracy on the California Coast," *Reason*, July, 1974, p. 18.
12 Ibid.
13 *Los Angeles Times*, December 9, 1973.
14 Ibid., August 19, 1973.
15 M. Bruce Johnson, op. cit., p. 19.

NOTES TO "BAKER'S DOZEN"
(CHAPTER EIGHT)

1 Benjamin A. Rogge, "The Case for Economic Freedom," *The Freeman*, September, 1963, p. 9.
2 Melvin D. Barger, "Socialism Seeks Its Own Level," *The Freeman*, June, 1974, pp. 356-57.
3 Will Durant, *Lessons of History* (New York: Simon and Schuster, 1968), pp. 59-64.
4 Will Durant, *The Story of Civilization III: Caesar and Christ* (New York: Simon and Schuster, 1944), p. 640.
5 Ibid., p. 642.
6 Ibid., p. 643.
7 Ibid., p. 644.
8 Ibid.
9 *U.S. News & World Report*, May 10, 1971.
10 Ibid.
11 Ibid.
12 Ibid., February 7, 1966.
13 Ibid., October 1, 1973.
14 Ibid., May 10, 1971.
15 Ibid., October 1, 1973.
16 Ibid., May 10, 1971.
17 Ibid.
18 Ibid., October 1, 1973.
19 Ibid., May 10, 1971.
20 *The Christian Science Monitor*, July 10, 1974.

21 Ibid.

22 Ibid.

23 "Reports & Comment: Sri Lanka," *Atlantic Monthly*, April, 1974, p. 20.

24 Ibid., p. 24.

25 *The Christian Science Monitor*, July 10, 1974.

26 *Atlantic Monthly*, op. cit., p. 26.

27 Ibid., p. 30.

28 Ibid., p. 32.

29 *The Christian Science Monitor*, July 10, 1974.

30 Melvin D. Barger, op. cit., pp. 360-61.

31 Erazim V. Kohak, "Being Young in a Post-industrial Society," *Dissent*, February, 1971, p. 31.

INDEX